T0265868

Aging Gracelessly

A Reluctant Agnostic's Investigation of the Holy Bible and Intangible Existence

Tom Bennett

Aging Gracelessly

A Reluctant Agnostic's Investigation of the Holy Bible
and Intangible Existence

GAUDIUM

Gaudium Publishing

Las Vegas ◊ Chicago ◊ Palm Beach

Published in the United States of America by
Histria Books, a division of Histria LLC
7181 N. Hualapai Way, Ste. 130-86
Las Vegas, NV 89166 U.S.A
HistriaBooks.com

Gaudium Publishing is an imprint of Histria Books. Titles published under the imprints of Histria Books are distributed worldwide.

Library of Congress Control Number: 2022942947

ISBN 978-1-59211-180-0 (hardcover)
ISBN 978-1-59211-219-7 (eBook)

Introduction

Although this book is not my first, it likely is my first serious book. Readers should take note that I will probably break a few established but somewhat minor (in my eyes) rules regarding the proper conventions for layout, grammar, citations, respect (bear with me), and punctuation. I do not consider myself an author... since my first book was self-published, and this one... at the time I am writing it, has not yet been published. I, therefore, declare myself exempt from the "normal" expression of thoughts in a writer's way. By this, I mean that English grammar enthusiasts will certainly condemn my freestyle as representative of a somewhat poor educational background and a blatant disregard for the literary taste of learned readers. I admit this to be true. I also thoroughly enjoy making up new words and using ellipses... with abandon.

I recently began to write a different book which sort of turned into this one... but yet wasn't. I realized, with a bit of disappointment, that it lacked a certain direction... my journal of random daily thoughts if you will. Perhaps not surprisingly, though, and as it progressed, it began to exhibit the symptoms of a recurring theme... namely my current, and admittedly ignorant, search for what I have come to believe is an essential need for spirituality of some, as yet, undetermined sort. I, therefore, decided to postpone, cancel, or at least interrupt regularly... my random thoughts in the interests of developing a more coherent book that hopefully will chronicle my unguided, but sincere, meanderings through the intangible universe of spirituality and/or faith.

This introduction is written before anything that follows. I felt a compelling need to post my disclaimers early on, but there is also this... I want to explain, for the benefit of those who seem to relish misunderstanding, that I have no outline to follow. There is no definite, or even concretely imagined, destination defined for the end of my spiritual journey. I have hopes, to be sure, that I will progress from the admittedly ignorant and needy psychological entity that I am... to a person of faith (in something) with at least a reasonable idea of who and what I am in the antiphysical side of existence. It is entirely possible, though, that since there are no tangible and provable answers to explain the spiritual side of human existence, I might very well find myself in an intangible maze of dead ends and heavily traveled paths to nowhere or anywhere. My intention, however, is to log my blind wanderings as I go... laying bare my emotional and intellectual discoveries as they fall on me. With luck, at the end of it all (if there is one), I will find a measure of validity in a spiritual path. I do not delude myself that there are answers or proofs in, or about, the spiritual domain... but there may indeed be validity in the mire. That much I see as possible... and worthy of investigation.

I will admit that I am a biased explorer. As a prime example of Midwestern mediocrity and low upbringing, I have not been subjected to avenues of spirituality that more worldly persons might find significant or worthy of consideration. Although I have pursued, in a very limited way, some of the concepts of Buddhism... by way of the Dalai Lama's teachings, I must admit to a considerable lack of knowledge of, or expertise with, that particular persuasion. I do understand, though, that Buddhism is not deity-based... which I find considerably more palatable (at this point) than other, deity-based faiths. I have even less experience or understanding of other faiths. I have, however, been splattered with bits and pieces of the Christian belief that were occasionally served me... whether rightly or wrongly or well-intentioned or not. Although there is a proliferation of literature on any subject readily available these days... with the internet and such, I have decided that my investigation of faith will be in the direction of Christian teachings... especially in light of the apparent fact that all of the various faiths claim validity, and all of them appear to be correct, and all of them seem to be worth fighting about. Why not, then, choose one... the one I am most familiar with, although admittedly quite ignorant of... and run with it.

Readers should also be aware of one or two important points that may not immediately be evident at first. Although my preparations for this book are nearly nonexistent, I did do two things in an effort to find a direction for the writings

that follow. First, after some considerable thought, I realized that I have no credentials for a meaningful study of Christian faith... although it occurs to me that
the study must come before the credential. One point, then, is that I will be con-
ducting a book-by-book report, if you will, of the King James version of the Holy
Bible... oh, not with a boring array of verse-by-verse criticisms, but certainly with
regard to occasional quotes that jump out at me in one way or another... or a
general overview Impression from my own personal perspective as "just some
guy"... and a self-avowed agnostic. And since I mention my agnostic status, I
should also explain, despite the ubiquitous idea that agnostic means something
similar to atheist, that I do not consider myself an atheist. I will explain this more
later, but for now, my point is that I intend to read the Bible, book-by-book, and
present my opinions regarding what I read... not only from my agnostic point of
view, but also as a PORTION of my investigations into spirituality and faith in
general. There will be more that I will consider besides what I find in the Bible...
and I will undoubtedly intersperse my journal-like discussions with occasional talk
of other things relating to what I call...my intangible existence, spirituality or its
pursuit.

The other preparatory measure was to actually purchase a new Bible... a most
peculiar experience for me since it came with a distinct feeling of being watched.
Read into it what you will.

So...it should be understood by now that I am not an author, I am not an
atheist, I am not an authority on anything, and I hardly know what I am doing at
this point. I probably should have been this concise earlier, but then I would likely
end up with an essay... which we all know only too well, won't impress anyone. A
book, however, demands a certain dedication to a cause... to the literary medium;
a concerted effort to produce a meaningful and lasting monument to my name,
however, well it happens to be accepted as a literary work. It is also more likely to
actually be read. Shall we see where this goes?

Aging Gracelessly

Peace
(4-26-11)

Oh, to set a lazy course from heavy hurts and worrisome woes
If only to say was to do, and to want was to have
Peace hides safely behind stubbornness and ignorance and grudges and grief
To look, alas, is not to see
To understand does not come free

So soon the tender heart is calloused and let go to fare on lessened love
To yearn for more is to wait for never and forever
The comfort of contentment earned is a possible promise hooked to hope
And wisdom is as wisdom does
If wisdom really ever was

November 10, 2012... Why Me?

A brief personal introduction is in order, I suspect. There can be no understanding of what I do if readers cannot understand who I am or where I have been. I have no wish to dig up smelly old memories and fling them at unsuspecting readers, but suffice to say that I am the product of a dysfunctional family... like so many others. We were poor. We found pride in our ignorances and shared them with abandon... with anyone prone to misdirection in their lives and questionable strength of character. I was raised in a chronic environment characterized by neglect and abuse and recurring suppression of personality. In short, I learned to hide myself inside myself so well that even I, myself, could not find all of me. What is worse is that I did not know it... it was completely "normal" to me. I learned to practice neglect from the neglect practiced on me. I grew into a victim of incessant negativity...

proficient in its dissemination to others. I regarded the world around me as I would measure its effect on me. I became an adult in body only. My intangible spirit got stuck in a mire of helplessness, hopelessness and a hazy, but very strong, feeling that something was missing. Looking back, I have come to the conclusion that, as a protective measure, I unwittingly buried a substantial portion of my own personality under a monstrous pile of barriers and armors that I found nearly impossible to understand, pick away at, or finally throw off the tender remains of a small boy who just wanted to be loved.

In the spring of 2003... and after fifty years, during a very low point in my life, I had my first major psychological epiphany. I slowly, very slowly, became aware that the world was not pushing me around. I was allowing myself to be led around in reaction to the pressures of the world. I can't express how profound this realization was to me. It grudgingly became clearer to me that the world, with all its idiosyncrasies, was just the world. It was I who allowed it to affect me. It did not force itself on me, it simply pushed and pulled at the seams of its own garments... and I got bumped by its occasional gyrations in my direction. It was how I reacted to it all that set that small boy on a course to burrow under all the safety layers and lose himself in a deep darkness that interfered with everything. It became normal to me as there was no other life to compare it with. I actually found some comfort in the bliss of ignorance which proved to be considerably easier to deal with than the terrific ordeal that digging out from it all turned out to be. Now, more than a decade later, although I have mostly "found myself" anew... and have struggled ceaselessly to discover my deficiencies and repair them, I still find one major mountain to climb... that of spirituality. In no small part, my climb will incorporate the spiritual gains and setbacks I am sure await me as I investigate the Bible and ponder my intangible existence during the writing of this book (I actually prefer to call it a discussion or journal).

I can't help but wonder how many others of a dysfunctional persuasion may be wallowing in a similar pool of stagnant ignorance and relentless emptiness of spirit. It is my sincere hope that in making my quest for a semblance of spiritual peace an open one... with everyone invited to experience it as I go... that I, and wishfully others, will find some measure of inner peace. If the salvation of my soul gets thrown in for good measure, I'm good with that.

November 11, 2012... Why Agnostic?

Thomas Huxley coined the term agnostic from the Greek a-gnosis which means "without knowledge". Although there seems to be some variation in how agnostic is defined, the "popular" meaning is that someone is noncommittal either way as to whether a deity exists or doesn't exist... and that it is not provable either way. The question of absolute certainty becomes of concern in the discussion. If I was to say, "Every man was once a boy," that would be an absolute certainty or truth because the only way a man can exist is by the growing up of a boy. But if I was to say, "I believe every man was once a boy," then I would be stating a belief, not a truth. It, therefore, is not an absolute certainty since no one can be absolutely certain about what I believe. Since faith relies on beliefs rather than truths, the doctrine of agnosticism becomes valid in that the belief in the deity is unprovable.

There apparently is, however, a sort of agnostic continuum, that throws a few complications into the soup. At one end, there is the agnostic atheist, who believes there is likely no deity... but that it can't be proven whether one exists or not. At the other end is the agnostic theist, who believes in the possible (or likely) existence of a deity... but acknowledges that its existence cannot be known with absolute certainty. Although there are others, somewhere in the middle is the apathetic agnostic who believes that since the existence of the deity cannot be known or proven, it really doesn't matter whether it exists or not... and there is no point pondering it at all. For the benefit of readers who may wonder, I will proclaim my somewhat shaky allegiance to the agnostic theist group. In the absence of a better explanation for the existence of all things, I am willing to accept that there is a possibility for some form of a God that bears responsibility in some way for the existence of the universe (or universes). Whether or not that God (whom I will refer to as simply "God") knows about me, or cares about me, is another issue.

I am an agnostic insofar as I reluctantly acknowledge the possible existence of A God... though not necessarily THE God. I also realize that the incompleteness of spirit I have experienced for over fifty years probably has much to do with the intangible side of my existence. The Bible is arguably the greatest book ever written (or assembled), and considering that the very subject of it could very possibly be the answer to my personal struggles, I would be a fool to lazily skip it and form a strategy for my continued, admittedly incomplete, existence without at least giving it some consideration. I cannot, however, rely on the biased help of my local pastor or atheist to respect my agnostic status as I slog through this quest for a more meaningful life. I, therefore, will make an honest and sincere effort to read the Bible on my own... and "in good faith", if you will... that is, with as much open mind as I can muster, and with as much written reaction as I can produce. With luck, I will not become disillusioned, ridiculed, assaulted or dismissed as just another crackpot trying to make a buck. ...and who knows... maybe I will find a valid enough reason to convert to a full Christian believer... as C.S. Lewis famously did. I am no C.S. Lewis, but I am a human being with a detectible physical presence and arguably real "intangible" existence... and I also possess the wherewithal to pursue my own personal significance (and salvation?). Whether my learnings here will be of benefit to others will be up to others to determine, but I have a great hope that this quest for knowledge and validity and spirituality will benefit me.

A true agnostic not only admits skepticism, but will harbor a desire to find some version of faith that is based, not on truths... only a fool would look for those, but on answers that lend validity to a way of thinking and believing. I consider myself, like Lewis, "reluctant" in that for most of my life I have had a serious disregard for faith-based thinking. It seemed very much like an exercise in futility and probably stupidity. Around the age of fifty, this changed. Without going into the reasons why, I will simply say that a powerful reassessment of my life began... complete with the beginnings of a new direction in thinking and a new way of dealing with everything. This life change did not happen overnight, and in fact, is still happening to this day. With every realization of how I used to be, I found a realization of how I should have been. It has been both, a curse and a blessing to experience.

So, when I speak about the answers I seek, I find another disclaimer is in order. Answers do not mean proofs. In my search for answers, I am looking for a measure of validity to justify a faith I have come to yearn for. I fully realize that I will never find proof for the existence or nature of God in my lifetime (…notice that last part?). I do, however, hope to find a reason to believe… and hopefully sooner than later. I have found that I am weary, very weary, of living in a physical world that, generally, ignores the intangible side of life to a considerable degree. I am aware of my consciousness, and I am fairly certain that my consciousness is not made up solely of electrical impulses. If that were true, I would probably have to pray to the light pole outside my window. I kind of like the idea that Pastor Mel mentioned, and which I had already considered… that our consciousness, feelings, thoughts, etc. may possibly live in another dimension that coexists with the ones most of us are aware of. Perhaps our brains have the ability to "link" with our minds somehow… through some undiscovered portal to this other dimension. Perhaps that is where the intangible, but wishfully real, manifestation of God lives. Wouldn't it be interesting if the strange and wondrous work of quantum physicists someday found the actual residence of God?

November 12, 2012… The Reality and Value of Me

A thought occurred to me. How does one take on something of magnitude like the Bible… or even the spiritual nature of human life, with little more than a nagging curiosity with which to form a valid opinion worthy of the respect, consideration and understanding of others? Can I rely on my Bachelor of Fine Arts degree for a measure of literary or intellectual credential? What is there about me that will develop credibility in my writings for the critical scrutiny of anyone?

I will go out on a figurative limb and say, with far too little prethought, that even without an Oxford education, an established literary reputation, or a friend in high places, that I consider myself to be absolutely equal to anyone who happens to encounter this rather unusual discussion I am having with myself… at least in one important respect: I am a human being. I rather doubt anyone could winningly dispute that claim… and as a human being, with all the intangible, spiritual, possibilities inherent therein, I find myself no less qualified or deserving to find inner peace as any other. I am, therefore I am okay... at least that is my opinion. A somewhat overpious zealot might argue that I don't have the right to inflict my underlearned thinking on a well-established and (perfectly) valid institution like (your religion here). But I, as a fellow human being, reserve as much right to express my thinking and findings as someone who feels strongly in other ways. As humans, we are equal in my eyes. As spiritual entities, we may not be... I concede that freely, but I defy anyone, zealot or not, to prove it.

It should be clear to readers, though, that although I am on a personal mission of spiritual discovery, I am absolutely NOT attempting to discredit or belittle anyone else's beliefs or faiths or biases. We are all welcome to our thoughts. If our own particular chosen manifestation of God finds a fault in that, I, for one, would be happy to address His concerns, with respect to my own shortcomings, directly. I leave, therefore, an open invitation for that discussion.

It has suddenly occurred to me as I write this that I seem to be full of disclaimers. Perhaps I harbor a fear of being killed by an overzealous adherent to one belief or another... or maybe I feel underqualified to produce a work of this type with no experience, no qualifications and no publisher's advance. Whatever excuse I might conjure, I do not mean to unnecessarily bore, or offend, readers with my probably trivial ramblings. I will try to behave.

Seriously though, just what might I mean by the "reality" of me? This is something I have put a considerable amount of thought into lately... and which, I am certain, many others have, as well. Being the admittedly ignorant person that I am, I will guess that many generations of philosophers have wrestled with this very question... probably with no more of an answer than I am likely to find. If I was a thinker of higher merit, I might research these various quests for spiritual enlightenment... and possibly find a path to follow, but unfortunately, I am not blessed with such merit and am relegated to find my own way in this intangible mire.

On the physical side, I think it can be said with a fair certainty that my body exists. I, at least, can see it and feel it and give excuses for it. But there is the question of what I call my intangible side. How can I hope to find a raison d'etre if I can't prove I even exist at all spiritually? It is sort of strange that I can sense, some-

how, that I have a conscious existence… and I can also sense the conscious existences of others, at least to an extent. I do, after all, know when someone is angry
with me. He or she is not angry with me because I can see their arms waving
around and their lips moving. There is an expression of feelings going on that I
am able to detect… and feelings are not a physical phenomenon (electrical pulses
aside). My emotions are real… although I, like everyone, am unable to provide the
absolute certainty required as proof. It appears to me that some sort of different
rules and criteria are needed to define and identify and validate the intangible side
of our existences. We know that dark matter exists in the universe… even though
we cannot see it and don't know what it is. We can measure its gravitational effects
on other objects with mass. Perhaps someone of a more intelligent persuasion will
someday discover a way to measure the effects of emotions thereby validating their
existence. It would be foolhardy to predict this possibility as impossible. The earth,
one might remember, was once flat.

So without opening an inordinately large can of worms, I might ask how anyone can define something like a conscious existence as real when reality, itself, has
a rather elusive definition. Do we discount our senses because what is sensed can't
be measured? Must we insist that the intangible be observed with our physical
detectors such as eyes or nerve endings? Are there other, as yet unfound, detectors
that we can place our faith in for the time being? In algebra, we supplant an unknown value with an "x"… and then try to find the "real" value of "x". Can we not
do the same thing with our spirits? Can there not be a spiritual algebra? Is it beyond
the comprehension of the human mind that its very existence might be detectable
or measured somehow someday?

I simply refuse to dismiss my intangible existence… as I'm sure virtually everyone would… for lack of tangible evidence for it. So, in the absence of tangible
proof… and in light of overwhelming, nearly universal acceptance that our conscious existences do indeed exist, I hereby declare the reality of me on an intangible
level.

As for the value that my intangible existence might have, although related to
the previous discussion, we now must think not only of the either/or proposition
as to whether I exist or not, but also how well I exist. This is the sticky area where

things like morality and faith come into play. And since morality and faith are as equally elusive to define as intangible existence, it becomes equally as challenging to accurately designate the value of a human being's spirituality. How, then, can we say something like, "He is a good Christian" when we actually have no measuring standard to make that claim? Where, along the imagined continuum of value, do we suddenly declare a person "good"? Who might be arrogant enough to assume that decisive right... with no substantive tools with which to build a valid argument?

I also refuse to dismiss my intangible value as a spiritual entity. As a self-avowed agnostic theist, I consider myself a member of the very same continuum as the "true believer" or the agnostic atheist, or possibly even the atheist. I am simply in a different spot on the line as the next person... and as I see it, it is not a question of good or bad, but rather of what I have learned or am willing to learn.

As a little sideline interlude of thought, I might mention that prior to my psychological "turn-around" in 2003, had I encountered a discussion such as the previous one regarding spiritual reality and value, I most certainly would have exclaimed, with the unmeasurable wisdom of a bore, that the whole thing is a tedious bunch of bullshit. "Why don't you just go have a nice cold beer and shut the hell up?" From my current perspective, I might say that even that questionable advice is really no more right or wrong or invalid than any I might come up with these days. I do, however, choose to choose my thoughts more thoughtfully lately.

November 13, 2012... An Unbiased Glimpse at Personal Bias

I have disclaimed that my ignorance in matters of faith will be self-evident as I make my way through the considerable challenge the Bible appears to be. It may also be of value for me to elaborate a bit on just what that might mean. My knowledge, such as it is, can probably be defined as my accumulated and retained thoughts on anything and everything... with a certain, undetermined, level of validity and accuracy.

I freely admit that I have preconceived notions about what I will find in the Bible... at least with respect to the Old Testament. Although I have not, as yet, read it, I do have a general idea about what it is about... or at least I think I do. Accordingly, it might be interesting to set up a before-reading/after-reading bias comparison. How do I view what little I know of the Bible NOW... compared to how I WILL view it when I have finished my critical reading of it?

I do admit that I have both biases and expectations about what I will read in the Bible... and how I will be affected by it. I will make an effort to explain as best I can. Regarding the Old Testament, I have come to believe that the basic idea behind it is to present the "inspired" word of God as a history, of sorts, detailing the significant events and teachings in the past that led up to the life of Christ... all of which were based on the FEAR of God. I have vague recollections of how some of the stories unfolded based on long-ago Sunday school lessons, and, of course, there have been many movies dealing with Bible stories... however good or accurate they might have been. It should be understood that until these very recent years, it never occurred to me that a person might actually think about the stories in a critical way and develop personal moralities based on them. I essentially considered the stories no more or less important or meaningful than Star Wars or the Iliad or Snow White. The source, significance, and salvation of my intangible soul just never mattered in the least. My oversimplified philosophy in my earlier years might be summed up something like this: If I can't see it, hear it, taste it or smell it, it just isn't worth wasting intellectual resources on... not that I possess any. My "turn around" about ten years ago changed all that forever.

A person would have to be brain dead to be completely ignorant about the life of Christ. Anyone born and raised in the United States would have been subjected to at least parts of His life story, teachings, morality, or significance. Some, more or less than others, would be brainwashed into certain beliefs. Others would acquire a reasonably balanced and worthwhile morality from the limited understandings they were "blessed" with. Still others (like me) would perpetuate the ridiculous biases of the undereducated and regrettably ignorant antithinkers that, to this day, proliferate unchecked essentially everywhere. The point is, though, that even I have heard of Jesus... and even I have an idea of what His significance is or can be. I believe it was C.S. Lewis who pointed out (to me) that the story of God and Jesus in the Bible is chronicled, compellingly, too historically to be disregarded as myth or unimportance. The New Testament, then, will be of special interest to me. Supposedly, as I understand it, it is based on the LOVE (not fear) of God.

At this very early stage of my search for spiritual meaning, I have questions... many questions. If the Bible is supposed to be the handbook for spiritual living... for anyone looking for peace and salvation, I very reasonably expect that I will find some answers (not necessarily proofs) that will validate at least SOME of the Christian dogma for me. Let it be understood that I WANT to find that validity. I WANT to be "saved". I do not trust the biases of others to learn about my own. This quest must be mine to make. In all honesty, I have a considerable fear that after these past ten years of critical self-evaluation... and after my sincere and looming investigation of the Christian way, I very possibly may find nothing of enough spiritual merit to me to give me the peace I seek. This would be very disappointing to me. I also hope to determine whether or not spiritual salvation is necessary or possible.

Another point of contention for me is the matter of ritual. It is quite obvious that ritual plays a very important part in the manifestation of faith... both on the sending side and the receiving side of "the message". I will have to hope that my ignorance and my genuine search for faith will somewhat excuse my almost blasphemous view of the ritual that I have encountered. I mean no harm in my reactions to these rituals... and if the salvation of my soul is of importance to "true believers", then my personal biases should be seen as my PERSONAL stumbling blocks... and, therefore, for me to deal with... and hopefully, forgivable.

My, perhaps, too pragmatic view of the rituals I see may very well have more significance and validity than I am aware of, but alas, at this early point in my search, I see profound and meaningless stupidities everywhere. Hopefully, readers will understand that I am not attempting to discredit nearly everything Christian... quite the contrary, I am laying bare my biases and likely mistaken beliefs and nagging ignorance in the interest of setting a baseline to begin my search for spiritual enlightenment. With an honest, concerted, effort in that direction... and with a little luck, I will be, at the end of it all, a different person... a better one.

I am perfectly able to address the intangible side of my existence in an intangible way. If I should choose to pray, I can do it anywhere I happen to be. I don't need a church. I don't need an evangelist's tent. I don't need a Sunday service... and, I'm betting, ten percent of my earnings won't make a single speck of a difference as to whether my soul is "saved" or not. I don't see any sense at all for a guy in a graduation robe to swing an incense thing around and speak Latin and light candles. It seems absolutely ridiculous to me that, by drinking a very small shot glass of grape juice and eating a chili cracker, I might symbolize anything more than wild imagination. I also refuse, to my dying days, to participate in what I call the stand up, sit down, kneel ritual. I realize these are strong words, but if I am to move from where I am now to where I hope I should be, honesty cannot be withheld in any way or compromised to any extent. In the spring of 2003, I made a vow to myself that I would never again be a liar. I have kept that promise to myself.

For many years, since Mason's class in World History in 1970, the number and characteristics of the various faiths and denominations of the world have perplexed me to no end. Surely if there is a God who can create an entire universe with the snap of His fingers, He, likely, could make His intentions and guidelines clear. They are not. There are far too many different religions in the world. How is a rational, thinking, person supposed to make the right choice when, without exception, each religion is right? The true believers of each are quite willing to kill to defend or propagate their faiths. Others will immolate themselves to make their point. Some will even go so far as to send out free little propaganda booklets.

Lately, in an effort to learn, I have begun to attend a local church. I have discussed my reasons for being there with the pastor, and have his "blessings". My thinking is that I would be remiss in my investigation if I were to judge the way others practice their faith without some firsthand experience on which to base my judgments. After several months, despite the impressive work of the pastor, I have found little redeeming value in what I have seen and heard. The music is wonderful (contemporary Christian songs), the sermons (when performed by the pastor) are excellent (He uses citations in his supportive claims), but, I have to say, some of the people appear to me to be overzealous pious quacks. They dance around waving flags and fall down in supplication and roll around in ecstasy. One person will suddenly blurt out a litany of gibberish as what is called "speaking in tongues"... and equally as "surprising", another person (always the same one) follows with an

English interpretation of what sounds like some sort of scripture or "message" from God. The length of the interpretation is often much longer than the original sputterings.

The parishioners justify to themselves that they have the power of healing and will "lay their hands on" anyone who is willing to get healed... although I have seen nothing more than the occasional falling backwards of the "healee"... conveniently into the arms of someone who has maneuvered himself into position behind him/her. They never collapse, they always tip backwards... obviously the correct way to feel the power of the Lord.

I have told myself that, despite these rather questionable behaviors, there might possibly be some value interspersed with the weirdness. The validity of the Christian faith is far too established and revered to be simply a confusing display of unnecessary and just plain strange behaviors. I, therefore, made a pact with myself that I would try to glean whatever I could of value from the proceedings and disregard the rest. To be sure, there IS a message. There are seemingly earnest people who appear to believe without all the vaudeville. I will earnestly continue to give it a chance.

There is one other real problem I see with the Bible which, hopefully, will be resolved by my reading of it. As I understand things at this point, the Old Testament tells the story of how God created the world (or whatever), made people, and tried to guide them via commandments that were to be obeyed on pain of death (the fear of God). The New Testament, likewise, is meant to be a "handbook" for living (if you will) based on God's love. This is probably an oversimplification, but it is, indeed, how I see things now. If, as I understand it, the Bible is the inspired word of God, it seems to me that it would be wrong for us mere mortals to interpret or dispute it. So why did He change His tactics? The old way apparently didn't work very well... as evidenced by Noah's flood (more on that after I read about it). It looks like God started things out a certain way... then when it didn't work according to His expectations, He wiped the slate clean and started anew. I am open to a discussion on this, but it appears to me that God couldn't make things work right the first time (why not?), changed His mind, and gave it another shot... which also, apparently, didn't work because He changed his tactics again and sent His

son down to try using the "love of God" method. Please excuse my blatant inso-
lence... or what I call critical thinking, but this sounds like trial and error to me.
Am I expected to absolutely accept, hook, line, and sinker, the uninterpreted word
of God when it plainly describes a God who operates on a trial and error basis?

Why would I decide to read a book that I plainly have serious validity issues
with? It is the only book that millions, or billions, of people all over the world
accept as the word of God... and they actually USE the book to PROVE what it
says. Supposedly, it is the word of God because it says it is the word of God. If
anyone in any other field of credentials and any other field of thought tried to use
that same tactic of reasoning as the basis for the validity of their ideas, they would
be laughed off the stage. But that very strategy is used openly and freely when the
Bible is used to "prove" the Bible. Any belief that can pull that off MUST have
something going on that I don't understand, but I, likely, will never understand
unless I investigate... and try to keep an open mind while I do. This, though, is
one of my most contentious concerns regarding the Bible.

It might be of some help, for any potential readers, to remember that much of
what I have written so far on these pages is as newly considered for me as it might
be for you. Although I have thought about many of the ideas that I have touched
on previously, I tend to think as I write. The very reason I am having what I call a
discussion with myself is that by writing my thoughts, I am able to organize and
analyze them in my mind to a much greater degree than I ever could if pressed to
speak them... or simply think them. Speaking...I would stumble and fall. Thinking...I would lose my way and forget where I have been or where I am going... or
worse, freeze up. Writing has always been my most successful means of communicating... even with myself.

In a way, I am addressing what I write to some possible future reader, but the
reality of it is that this book really is both, a very sincere and honest search for a
valid spiritual path, and a way of cleaning out the junk in my attic and replacing
it with well-considered items that actually may be of real use as I live out the rest
of my life. But, failing that, I might possibly hone my typing skills.

If this quest of mine... and this book... is eventually seen by others, there is every likelihood that well-meaning solicitors of questionable sanity or various denominations will want to exert their influence to hasten the continuance or completion of my conversion. I will declare now, in a most unambiguous way that I will reject all attempts. This search is mine. Its results will be mine. If my efforts appear misguided to others, those same others have my reasoned condolences. If I do, indeed, accomplish my goal of finding validity for a spiritual path that works for me, I will be quite thrilled to share my experience with anyone who expresses an interest, but I also promise (hand on Bible) that I will not become one of those solicitors. I have my reasons... please respect them.

November 14, 2012... In the Beginning (Genesis)

There will undoubtedly be those who will take issue with what might be considered my stupid, irrelevant, or unnecessary thoughts concerning "the beginning". I feel, though, that I have made it abundantly clear that the ideas I lay upon these pages are nothing more than my own personal discussions with myself. I also will ask readers to forgive my occasional lack of proper citations. It is not meant to be a sign of disrespect or an attempt to circumvent credit where credit is due. I really just don't see the point in citing every small passage when I am obviously discussing a topic from a specified section of the Bible. So let me say, in earnest, that I consider the Bible to be one of the greatest books ever written or compiled... probably THE greatest. Whether I consider it a valid source for the understanding of God and the salvation of my soul is another matter which I will save for later when I have actually read it. So with that, let me begin.

Though I don't mean to give the impression that I will pick apart the entire Bible word-by-word, I do have a bit of a problem with the first three words. I fully realize that the Old Testament, at least, was purportedly the inspired word of God. As I understand it... and I might very well be wrong... the story of creation was (sort of) put into the heads of Moses and others so that they might write it all down for posterity. Whether or not any of it is fair game for interpretation is a matter that others can determine. As I see it, if God meant for us mere humans to know something, He would undoubtedly let us know in no uncertain terms, would He not? After all, why inspire a handbook for living that is ambiguous when it will be required that we completely and promptly obey...or die? I have a strong feeling from what little I already know about the Bible that this issue will be a recurring concern of mine throughout my humble quest for understanding.

So in the beginning there was...etc. In the interest of clarity, I think we can assume (interpret?) the "beginning" refers to the beginning of the earth and "heavens". I'll call it the universe. Setting aside the work of quantum physicists who are beginning to see evidence that there may actually be an infinite number of universes, supposedly God created our little corner of the universe at the very least... in the beginning. So if there wasn't a universe before the beginning, where exactly was God? Heaven you say? Where's that? And if Heaven was somewhere or everywhere or whatever, was the beginning really the beginning? It seems to me that in the real beginning God must have rode into town and set up shop in some, as yet undetermined, way. I have heard people say that God is eternal. He was always there or here or somewhere. Well then, I have to wonder who or what created God? If He was already and always "out there", then what might He have been doing with himself for the eternity or so that He must have existed before the beginning? And how can there have been a beginning if there was an eternity before it? Okay, I'm being a bit facetious, but if we assume that God created OUR universe in the beginning, then don't we also have to ask ourselves what right we have to make that assumption? There is that interpretation question again.

I realize that some of my ignorant understandings will seem tedious and even offensive to some people. I must admit that I have already caused a small amount of animosity in my own familiar circles because my agnostic probings make certain true believers uncomfortable. It is only after I fully explain that I am not looking for absolute answers or proofs so much as a measure of spiritual validity that others see that I am earnest in my quest for spiritual understanding. I try to make it clear that I respect the views and beliefs of others as much as my own... especially in light of the fact that I cannot validate or discredit the belief of others any more than I can my own.

November 16, 2012... Who Took Notes?

On the first day, God said, "Let there be light." He then divided the light into day and night. On the fourth day, God put "lights" in the firmament of the heaven to divide it (again?) into day and night. There was a greater light to rule over the day (the sun) and a lesser one (the moon) to rule over the night. He also made the stars.

My experience as an amateur astronomer tells me that our sun IS a star... it just happens to be a really close one. So if our star provided the light of day... beginning on the fourth day of creation, what exactly was the light created on the first day? According to the inspired word, the stars and the sun (same thing) were made on the fourth day. There may be an inspired answer that I have as yet to encounter, but at the moment I find I have to assume (interpret?) that there was simply "light" of some sort... that apparently wasn't radiating from anything. It was simply there. Well alright then. If a God is able to create, with the figurative snap of His fingers, the universe, then it shouldn't be difficult to accept that His light doesn't have to radiate from a light source. Let's call it a work in progress.

I find there are many, many passages in Genesis that I find disconcerting, to say the least. I will not attempt a fruitless discussion of them all... though I will think about a few. In Genesis 3:22 there is a direct quote from God, "Behold the man has become as one of us..." Who is "us"? Throughout my pitiful life, I have been led to believe that there is only one God... and now God himself, in a direct quote... and in His infinite and omniscient wisdom, says "us". This is the inspired word of God. Who is "us"?

There is also the matter of the serpent, the tree of life, and the tree of knowledge of good and evil. It has been suggested to me that the two forbidden trees were placed in the Garden of Eden as a test for Adam and Eve. This, though, is not stated in Genesis that I have seen. And although it seems a likely enough explanation, it also raises a couple of questions that I now wrestle with. If God strictly forbade Adam and Eve from eating the fruit of the tree upon pain of death, why did He feel the need to test them... knowing as He surely must have, being God, that they would do it? If His ultimate plan was to send them out of the Garden to become farmers, why did He create the Garden in the first place? I should think Him perfectly capable of just creating Adam and Eve down at the farm.

The tree of life, strangely, appears to have gotten ignored after the tree of knowledge fiasco. God, Himself, declares that the fruit of the tree of life would endow the eater with everlasting life. No one, however, seems interested in that. Had I been Adam, having been threatened with certain death by God, Himself (which didn't happen), and after being caught and condemned... with nothing much more to lose, would certainly have made a proverbial bee line to the tree of life and partaken of its fruit in fairly short order. That everlasting life would have come in very handy around that time, I should think. But since none of that happened, and to my knowledge, nothing regarding the tree of life happened subsequently, why was it there? Did God not know which tree Adam and Eve might eat from? Might it have been an easier test if there was only one tree? The apparent reason for the story, in the first place, is of some curiosity. If God made Adam in His image, why didn't He know Adam would do what He, Himself, likely would have done? Who, exactly, is supposed to benefit from the telling of the story... farmers? Why didn't God simply make Adam right? If God was so adamant about obedience in the Old Testament, why did He create people who would disobey? ...and then get mad at them when they did? This, too, will come up again, I fear.

With respect (hardly) to the serpent, I really do not know where to start. Why? Why? Why? Part of the test, you say? Well alright, let's go with that. In the interest of understanding, l will review. God, knowing exactly what He was doing, created a talking serpent to temp Eve into eating the forbidden fruit so that she, in turn, could temp Adam into eating it... knowing by the promise of God that they would die... but also know of good and evil... apparently as they were dying. What good is the knowledge of good and evil if, "...you shalt surely die"? The talking serpent also proclaimed that if they ate the forbidden fruit, they would become, "like gods." Gods? Plural? Didn't he mean, "like God"? Now it appears the serpent had some confusion as to the actual number of gods, as well. This quest for spiritual enlightenment and validity is, perhaps, starting off on a strange and perplexing path... despite the supposition that these "stories" are the inspired word of God.

After Cain slew Abel, he told the Lord that he didn't know where Abel was. He (Cain) also told God that with his banishment from the garden of Eden, anyone he might meet would kill him. He then fled to the land of Nod where he found a wife. Although I have issues with many more things than what I have just mentioned, I will address these few. Cain killed his own brother... so he was a murderer, and then blatantly and directly lied to God's face... so he bore false witness, and after virtually one line of worry, God told Cain that He would mark him that anyone who killed him would face the wrath of God. These days, it might be construed as harboring a criminal. And just who were these other people that would kill Cain if he might encounter them? Assuming Adam and Eve were the first people on the earth... and Cain and Abel were the next humans, who were the others and where did they come from. Where did Cain's wife come from? Where, in fact, did the land of Nod come from? Let me guess…interpretation will answer all.

November 19, 2012... Genesis or Genocide

The entire story of Noah and the flood is preposterous in my view. I am sure our ubiquitous interpreters will have a field day with me and my narrow-minded and somewhat blasphemous take on this, but, at least in my eyes, none of it makes any sense at all. Is the Bible the inspired word of God? Do we interpret it? If so, are not my interpretations as valid as anyone else's? If not, are we to seriously accept an entirely unfounded, unbelievable, and unnecessary story as the absolute truth? The very premise of the story is that God created the earth and everything on it, became disappointed in His own work, and then decided to wipe the slate clean and start over. Setting aside the assumption that God created the land of Nod so that the murdering liar, Cain, would have a place to settle down and start a family, it seems incredibly unbelievable that a God who could create life with the snap of his fingers, would bother to make it rain for forty days and forty nights in order to "undo" his work. I realize that God supposedly moves in mysterious ways, but I hardly find it appealing to accept the crazy work of a deity that would kill all of the children, squirrels, butterflies, trees, and everything else that lived on the earth because things weren't going the way He thought they should. Is it so terribly difficult to imagine that He could have killed only the bad guys? And finally, when Noah sent the dove out after ten or eleven months, it came back with an olive leaf... presumably plucked from one of the dead trees that God killed.

I do not want to misrepresent myself as simply against the Bible... especially at this early point in my reading of it. There will be more discussion on the order of what has preceded, but it occurs to me that if my only response (so far) is totally negative, then I necessarily must have a closed mind that is unwilling to find any redeeming quality in any of it. I do not wish to make my search for spirituality that kind of quest.

It appears to me that the Old Testament, and Genesis in particular at this point, was "inspired" and written to lay down a basis for understanding the workings of God with respect to a particular group of people... the chosen ones... the children of Abraham. It is a wonderful story... however questionable I may deem it. A people without formal and consistent schooling might find the story of Genesis compelling and powerful... and I have to assume the people of Abraham were just that. It is, therefore, understandable that these chosen people would find real significance and value in such a tale. I will give the inspired writer (Moses?) credit for crafting a really great story.

My local pastor has suggested to me that the story of "God's people" in the Old Testament only tells the tale of what transpired regarding the Hebrew people. In his "interpretation", many of the things I have questions about are not explained because they have no direct meaningful part to play in the explanation of God's work. The land of Nod, for instance, is not explained because it simply doesn't matter in the context of the chosen people's dogma... though I have to ask myself, if God created the world and everything on it, He obviously created the land of Nod, as well. Why... if it didn't matter? Is God to be seen as a deity who does unnecessary things?

There is one other concern I have regarding the "chosen people". It is likely, I suppose, that this will be addressed later in the Great Book, but my question at this point is this: If there were created other peoples on the earth (besides the chosen ones)... that apparently didn't (or don't) matter to the story of the workings of God, is it possible for the NON-chosen ones to be accepted into the kingdom of

Heaven? I have to assume that, through Jesus, anyone can be "saved", but at least in this early part of the Bible, this question does not seem to be addressed. It appears to me that the people of Nod were simply "zoned out" of Heaven. Too bad, so sad. Is God, then, also to be seen as a deity who plays favorites?

There are also a few concerns with Abraham. First, he marries his own sister, then he has drunken sex with his two daughters, makes a deal with God that if he circumcises all the males of his household and family forever... he will be the father of many nations. I fully realize that the customs and norms of society change over time, but I find it very disconcerting that a revered man of God... one CHOSEN by God explicitly for His purpose... should be one who, these days, would be put away for a very long time... and discredited as a deviate and a perpetrator of sexual mutilations. Do we not abhor this very kind of disfigurement as it applies to young girls in our modern world of today? Would we not severely condemn a man convicted of such deeds today... despite his claims that the Almighty made him do it? Or, perhaps, we might find him not guilty by reason of insanity.

November 21, 2012... Another Reminder...

I am reading the Bible, not in reverence to its message, but as a potential source of validity for the Christian dogma from which I hope to find personal significance, a path to inner peace, and even spiritual salvation... whether that is possible or not. Readers should not confuse my critical responses to my readings as an atheist-like condemnation of an entire worldwide faith... or the fact that I am reading the Bible in the first place...as an indication that I am on a path to giving myself to God. The truth of it, if I may be so blunt, is that I have, for most of my life, felt "lost" spiritually... and I am quite weary of it. Although I have made a considerable attempt to find information regarding how to read and interpret the Bible, I have found nothing of an unbiased nature to help me in my search. Every source, including the self-proclaimed "unbiased" ones, attempts to influence how I should or should not accept or interpret the Great Book. I, therefore, find that I must reiterate my right to interpret as I can... as all the others, likewise, do. I see no reason to separate my interpretations from those of others as somehow lacking or unqualified or uneducated. The Bible, if I understand its intended purpose, is no more or less meant for one person than another. Its meaning is as much for me to discern as it is for others.

I admit to my ignorance... and to some extent, revel in it. As I stated earlier somewhere, I would rather be an honest and ignorant fool than a biased and arrogant fake. Fool though I am, my heart, I believe, is sincere... and if God really DOES care about me, and see me wallowing in my personal mire, He will, if He is what I have come to expect, open His arms to me despite my rather lengthy and perhaps distasteful meanderings.

I suppose I should also clarify the fact that although I am noting the date on which I begin reading each book of the Bible, I am actually taking it in snippets and writing about the various parts over the course of days or even weeks. I will not skip any of it... and I don't intend to skip around taking things "out of order"... though I have come to understand that parts of it were not meant to be included in any particular order. I will read all of it little-by-little, from beginning to end, and comment as I proceed through it... and all of my observations will be noted as I encounter them... my comments written as I think of them.

November 23, 2012... The Joy of Sects

Although I have a copy of the King James Bible at my side as I write this, I will also confess that I am listening to the NEW King James version on my car CD player, as well. As I listen (in those previously mentioned snippets), I refer to the original KJ version to verify that what I think I heard is in fact what I did hear.

I have heard comments in the past about sex... and incest... in the Bible, but because of my admittedly ignorant revulsion of all things religious (in the past), I simply ignored all of it as something others might deal with more appropriately. Today, I encountered the story of how Jacob, the son of Isaac, found a wife. Without repeating what has been widely read by more capable readers than me, I will say that there does, indeed, appear to be what we in these modern times would call rampant incest. Jacob bargains with his own uncle for Rachel to become his wife. Good 'ol uncle La'ban, in his questionable wisdom, instructs his other daughter Le'ah to secretly (?) lay with Jacob... who doesn't catch on until the following morning... and then wonders at the dastardly deception. La'ban then gives Le'ah to Jacob as a wife, and although Jacob is in love with Rachel, he "goes into her" anyway and produces six sons... obviously consolation prizes. Le'ah also offers her maidservant to lay with him, as well. Then Rachel gets into the act and offers her maidservant, too... and Jacob goes into her. Then Jacob gets Rachel pregnant, as well. It is beginning to get abundantly clear what the Lord meant when he promised Abraham that his "seed" will multiply like the stars in the heavens.

I do not want to seem overcritical of what may very well have been the sexual norms over three thousand years ago, but it does strike me that the chosen people of God were not only blessed but also blessed with a few disconcerting perks. I am a bit perplexed, that the ultimate book of morality portrays the chosen people of God (Abraham and Jacob, in particular... so far) as sex-crazed, incestual, perpetrators of drunken sex and sexual disfigurement. If we were, indeed, created in God's image, I have to ask myself if this is the kind of thing that He does in his spare time?

December 22, 2012... Influence and Bias

By the dates recorded here, it can be deduced that I have been lacking lately... in a regular continuance of thought. This is not actually the case, but I will explain my missing month of journal writing. First, I will confess that I actually lost the portion of the audio Bible I have been listening to. It is now found. I have also been pondering the inevitable influences and biases I encounter daily... regarding the Christian belief. There are three in particular that I will mention in an effort to underline a bit of the world I face while stumbling through my intangible spiritual maze.

I mentioned earlier that I have been attending a local church with my "believer" wife on the Sundays that I am available to go. She (my wife) has been a rather precious resource for me during my search for spirituality... despite the inherent dysfunction that I unwittingly brought into our adult lives. With her (somewhat recent) commitment to wholehearted belief, I am experiencing firsthand how Christian thinking can benefit people. By this, I mean to say that through her

heartfelt acceptance of Christ, my wife is finding a way to deal with past unpleasantness... and, I can only hope, an eventual forgiveness for my unintended failings.
One of my most pressing wishes is that I can find some measure of redemption in
her eyes... along with an acceptance that I am no longer, and never can be, the
person I used to be. I find that, although it is difficult for anyone, it is much easier
for me to see the intangible side of me... than it is for her. I give her unbounded
credit for trying.

One facet of this influence on me that I find disheartening is the inexplicable
tendency that believers seem to have to try and "pass on" the joy and salvation they
think they have found to others (me). Although I can appreciate their well-mean-
ingness, it seems a convenient way for a religion to self-perpetuate when believers
are encouraged to "do God's work". What is troublesome to me is that we pitiful
humans... even the chosen ones... are notorious for our repeated and disgraceful
failure to represent God with any real integrity. History, not I, will illustrate this
numerous times with familiar results and very disappointing regularity. I find it
more than a little disturbing that these historically unqualified, self-proclaimed
(arrogant?) believers can assume the responsibility of helping me to enlightenment
in God. I love my wife dearly, but I am quite capable of sorting out what is meaningful to me, worthy of my investigations, and valid enough to me to make a final,
eventual, commitment in spirit... just as she did. It was, after all, MY idea to seek
out a spiritual path for myself. I do not need "a push" in the direction someone
else is going... even when I may very well go the same way. I will find my own way.

The second influence I have encountered is one I also mentioned earlier. Pastor
Mel is somewhat of an enigma to me... mainly due to my ignorance of his life,
though I have great respect for the man at this point. I know very little of his story,
but I do recognize thoughtfulness and respect, and intelligence when I see it. Despite the obligatory ritual and vaudeville that I find quite unnecessary at the Sunday service, the sermon portion of the proceedings is impressive and meaningful
to me. Mel's approach is to select a small and specific message from the Bible...
perhaps part of a continuing theme, and then sentence-by sentence... and even
word-by-word... he will explain what it means in the context of his theme and the
overall message of the Bible and the teachings of Jesus. I am particularly gratified

that he does not simply give his opinion... or interpretation, but instead cites various sources of interpretation... complete with on-screen quotes with credits. Although he obviously uses the cited quotes to illustrate his message, it is refreshing to experience a sermon that is more of a school-like lecture of learning than biased brainwashing of traditional dogma. There is no "believe or go to Hell" approach. Instead, he extends an invitation for all to exercise their powers of acceptance in the interest of joy. Believer or not, I can find no fault with that. He also has considerable skill with a Telecaster.

Both of the two influences I have mentioned so far in today's journal entry are believers. The third is not. Bible enthusiasts will undoubtedly take exception to my allowance of antiBible thinking into my discussion, but as I see it, an unbiased study of spirituality... by a self-avowed agnostic... MUST include other points of view... if for no other reason than to get a more balanced perspective. It would seem, though, that a balanced perspective is not particularly palatable to a believer who is committed to ONE way of thinking, but that is not me. I am agnostic and, therefore, open to possibilities.

Although many people would vehemently discredit the internet as an accurate or valid source of information, I find that, as in real life, there are many (mostly biased) views on every subject to be found there... and it is, therefore, no more or less valid as a source of information than the everyday real world. The trick is to sort out what is thoughtful and reasonable from all points of view... and form an opinion based on personal preferences and choices, not the ravings of any one particular internet source. This doesn't seem to be different than how we would operate in the real world when we form opinions.

I recently encountered an enigmatic, atheist on YouTube that I found entirely interesting, refreshingly intelligent, bold, and honest... and who at least made an effort to respect potential listeners/watchers by presenting opinions in a clear and concise, albeit biased, way. I will not mention a name. This person was much more thoughtful than most, and demonstrated a very logical and compelling argument for atheism that even a practiced thumper would have difficulty disputing. Many of the points that were presented in the videos are also ones I have addressed earlier, but I can say with the utmost respect that this person had an admirably plain, disarmingly direct way of communicating that anyone of reasonable intelligence would find envious. I bring this up because my search for spirituality, according to my own guidelines, necessarily requires the consideration of different views and open-ended possibilities. How could I possibly declare Christianity as valid if I had not considered what else might be possible? A one-sided argument is not an argument at all. It is a simple bias. If I am to be biased in my intangible beliefs, I prefer my bias to be a mistake... and not a blatant and arrogant disregard for alternate possibilities. This internet person, although at times somewhat arrogant in an atheist sort of way, was stunningly compelling to listen to... and I have to say (at this point), much more convincing than just about anyone I have experienced so far. This does not mean I am becoming an atheist. I am not abandoning my spiritual quest. I fully intend to find some sort of spiritualism that will work for me... whether it involves Christian dogma, atheism, Buddhism, or dark chocolate.

December 23, 2012... Experiential Learning vs Lectured Learning

It has been my experience that experience really is the best teacher... at least with respect to the intangible side of our existence. That is to say that in my own life I have found myself to be resistant to criticism... constructive or not, and repeatedly have demonstrated how resistant I can be in accepting it. To be more specific, I will admit to being told many times in the past that I didn't seem to understand that I was dishonest and disrespectful and really not very compassionate. I am not proud of this truth. To make a long story short, I will simply say that I eventually visited the lowest place in my life... where I, fortunately, found a stripped-down, easier to see, me. I realized, with considerable disappointment, that much of what I had been told about me for decades...was true. I was a liar. I was ignorant. I was inconsiderate and stubbornly inaccessible. I learned these things NOT when they were told to me, but when I had gotten to a point where there was nothing left but the truth. The experience of going through my own personal hell enabled me to finally open my eyes and begin to see what was there all the time. It is only with the humble realization that my own biggest problem was me... that I was, at last, able to start digging my way out of the bottomless pit I had allowed myself to fall into. In short, I began to look inward as well as outward.

During the past several years, I have been fortunate to find strengths that I had not imagined in myself. Strengths are good... when they are applied in positive ways, and although it has taken far too much time to discover my idiosyncrasies and strengths, it is comforting to right some wrongs now and avoid a few mistakes that would, otherwise, have unfolded as in the past. I am not stupid, though... I fully realize that learning never ends for anyone who is willing to learn... and anyone who is NOT willing to learn, whether experientially or not, will suffer along with those who they encounter.

I do not mean, by this discussion, to say that lectured learning doesn't work. On the contrary, it works very well when the learner is open to the learnee. As I said earlier, "experience is the best teacher"... not the only one. Now that I have endured the experience of learning (the hard way), I find I can more easily accept the learning I receive by lecture. Where I was closed to outside suggestions at one time, I have now accepted that my own blindness is the reason for my inability to see... and I am willing, and even hungry, for learning now... even when it may be disconcertingly about me. Tell me what I should know about myself. I will listen. Allow me to learn from my own mistakes. I will persevere. Recognize that I am a work in progress (as we all are), and I will extend the same consideration to others.

December 27, 2012... The End of the Beginning

I believe I stated a short time ago that I started reading the Bible anew so that I could comment, book-by-book, on what I find there. I have now completed my second reading (listening) of Genesis... and can say, with trepidation, that I found it a fairly fascinating story that I, for one, would not think of taking to heart. I am quite sure that with the benefit of unambiguous belief, I would be suitably impressed with the great power and fearful expectations of God... but as an agnostic, I am not bound by an irrational and unjustified, uncompromising belief based on what I have been led to believe is the "inspired" word of God. I did not read anywhere in Genesis that Genesis is inspired by anyone. Perhaps that will come later, but at this point, I must admit a certain disappointment in the great book... or at least the great chapter. I do, however, fully intend to give the entire book a chance. I simply cannot suppose, in my admitted ignorance, that a very large portion of the world's population might be wrong about the Bible... and that skeptics (like me) or atheists are right. There is more to this than meets the eye... and I will investigate further.

December 28, 2012... Nitpicking Exodus

Since I have chosen to take the UNguided tour through the Bible... without benefit of unbiased interpretation (which doesn't seem to exist)... I will undoubtedly make mistakes... either in interpretation or simply in recollection. Obviously, I do not mean to nitpick at established and revered scripture, but I do feel I have a responsibility to myself to read cautiously and as critically as I can. I realize that I simply cannot analyze every line I read... I do not consider myself capable or qualified enough to masterfully review each and every small detail I encounter as I progress. So again, I will discuss with myself a few points of concern as I catch them along the way. I am reasonably certain, though, that I will as likely miss other points worthy of critical examination. I will also undoubtedly seem somewhat ignorant of what might be considered well-known or established meanings derived from allegory... despite the fact that I consider such interpretations little more than guesswork. I apologize to those who disagree, but I find allegory groundless exercises in speculation.

Early in Exodus, I think it is 2:18-21, Re-u'el gives Moses his daughter, Zippo'rah, for a wife... who bears him a son. Shortly thereafter, in 3:1, Moses keeps "the flock of Je'thro his father in law". It appears that, in the time span of only a half dozen or so verses, Re-u'el has changed his name to Je'thro. I read this three times to make sure I actually did read correctly. Now I find myself questioning the "inspired" word of God as purportedly written by Moses, himself... when he doesn't seem to know who his father-in-law is.

There is also a brief rundown of the lineage leading to the birth of Aaron and Moses... whose father married his own aunt. Why, exactly, were these the chosen people of God?

Moses throws down his staff and it becomes a serpent to make Pharaoh fearful, but then Pharaoh's magicians throw down theirs... which also become serpents (though they were promptly swallowed by Moses' serpent). I know of the miracle of God in making the staff of Moses turn into a serpent, but who, exactly, is backing the magicians? God plainly states (to Moses) that He will harden Pharoah's heart several times... prompting Moses to display the various "miracles" provided by God. I am perplexed about this. God makes Pharoah's heart "hard", and then punishes him for having a hard heart. He then (through Moses) punishes all of Egypt... including all the plants and animals and fish... which apparently must have played an unspecified part in the persecution of the Hebrew people. In fact, He killed the cattle twice... once with the wave of a hand (Exodus 9:6), and some of them again with the raining fire and hail (Exodus 9:19). And then, just to be sure, He killed some of them again (Exodus 12:29) via the angel of death during the first Passover. One should not be found lacking when punishing the despicable cattle, it seems.

It occurs to me that another disclaimer is in order. One might wonder at my audacity in passing judgments on the great book... being the self-avowed, ignorant, agnostic that I consider myself to be. Why should any opinion of mine have any merit at all to others who believe in it? It came to me today (December 31, 2012) that a small explanation might be of some help. One of the very most basic reasons for my writings here is that I wish to take on this search for spiritualism... complete with a critical review of the Bible... from the perspective of...just some guy. I have been thinking, recently, that the overwhelming majority of Bible readers... or proponents, for that matter, are laypeople who are not learned scholars or scriptural experts. They are what I often refer to as "real people"... who read the Bible because they always read it, or because someone MADE them read it as a child, perhaps. Maybe it is someone who was lost and now is found... or possibly someone who has read it by way of snippets absorbed in church over the course of a lifetime. Believers, it appears to me, often validate their own belief by virtue of their belief in the Bible... whether they have actually read it or not, and even more importantly... whether they have actually attempted to understand it or not. This is where I stand apart from many I have encountered. I am trying to understand the Bible... even if I don't happen to accept everything I read. I seriously doubt I might find any measure of understanding without reading it. Likewise, I doubt I could understand it, as others claim to, without absorbing it on my own personal terms and without the assistance of expert adherents... just as others do. Although I have my own biases, I reserve the right to use them as I choose... just as others do. Perhaps I will end up a believer... perhaps not. However this rather tedious and challenging quest unfolds, I will undoubtedly be considerably more qualified, having read it, to stand behind my experiential Biblical leanings. My goal... despite what others may find arguable... is to find validity for my beliefs. I simply wholeheartedly refuse to operate on faith alone without a reasonably valid reason for doing so.

There are a couple of things that I wonder about... not being of a particularly scholarly persuasion. One concerns the perplexing adventures of unleavened bread. I have come to have a rather vague understanding that the occasionally required unleavened state of the bread may symbolize the hasty exodus made by the beleaguered Hebrews. That is well and good, I guess, but I began to wonder about the reason for this symbolism at all. I ask myself...why would God REQUIRE, as part of the sacred covenant, that the chosen people throw away their yeast for a week or so? Is it just me, or does this sound more than a little ludicrous? I cannot help but wonder what my wife would say if I suddenly required her to throw away all the ketchup or else our marriage is off and I might even kill her. It sounds the same to me. Surely a powerful God capable of creating an entire universe, with sentient life, would have absolutely no concern whatever... whether someone, chosen or not, might have some yeast in the house. Symbolism or not, it sounds wholly silly.

Another disconcerting symbolic curiosity concerns the phenomena of the firstborn. The birthright of the first-born son, the killing of the first-born male lamb, the redemption of the first-born donkey... first-born this, first-born that; is this really all necessary? I fully realize that times are different now, but can it be that no one in Biblical times noticed that there seemed to be myriad somewhat unnecessary and arguably weird practices being put forth? Throughout our current modern society, we see countless examples of absurdities that quickly fade from mainstream acceptance. Were so few books written about these things that no one thought to think them out? Could not the learned and blessed writers of the Bible sort out the questionable dictates from the genuinely useful ones and edit with a measure of "common sense"? It seems to me that a poor person... and I have to think there were a few back then... might have some difficulty producing a firstborn calf for sacrifice, if he didn't happen to own one... believer or not. Sacrificing, itself, seems an inordinately strange practice to require of a people living in hardship. The fear of God is one thing, but I wonder if He thought out his strategy for the reasonable and sensible existence of His people very well.

January 3, 2013... Blind Faith vs Independent Thought

It has been suggested by those who are close to me that I might find considerably more comfort and peace in spirit if I were to simply surrender my concerns and skepticism regarding the validity of God (to Jesus) and begin enjoying the life I claim to desire. My independent thought, it seems, is my most interfering impediment to my own spiritual contentment. I have gotten into my own way... in other words. At first glance, I find this entirely narrow-minded and simplistic... and probably just plain wrong. But then, in all honesty, I do see some...well...validity to this possibility. If I were to suddenly become so weary of my spiritual yearnings and deficiencies that I chose to forgo my search for information and simply give in to a certain way of thinking... give myself to Jesus, for example, would I not immediately begin to accept and enjoy what is often called grace? I believe that is entirely possible... and I believe people do exactly that all the time. But I also DO have a problem with this process. If I was created by God to be the person that I am... complete with skepticism and independent thought, then I have to think I was meant to question things. What sense would it make for God to give independent thought and skepticism to people and then condemn them, or ignore them, for using it? It brings to mind the repeated offenses of the Hebrew people during the exodus... in doubting God's wisdom and deeds... or forgetting the miracles performed for their benefit. Those very same "chosen" people were created in His image, given their deficiencies with the full understanding by God that they would misuse them, and then were punished several times for doing it.

I have to ask myself... why would God feel the need to "test" His people at all. He surely knew all along, and from the very beginning, that they would fail Him over and over. And to render this all down to some even more basic level, what is the point of having a "chosen" people at all? What does "chosen" mean? Does it mean that these people (the Hebrews/Jews) are the only ones on Earth that can find salvation and sit with God? If so, why do the rest of us exist? Does the Pigmy in South America suffer in Hell for eternity when he doesn't even know about God at all? Does the ignorance of God equal the rejection of Him? Does the rejection of Him exclude a person from some future redemption? If our souls exist after death, can we not find redemption at some point after we die? If God is interested in our intangible existence, why did He give us physical bodies at all? If our souls truly are (or can be) immortal, what is the significance of having ninety years or so of baryonic existence? If I have these very questions bouncing around in my physical brain, can I simply ignore them and start enjoying grace forever? Since I have the ability to think on my own, and can choose to ignore my own thoughts if I wish, can I also choose NOT to ignore my independent thoughts and pursue a sincere search for understanding the intangibleness of life without being penalized for doing so?

One might, at this point, wonder at my description of myself as an agnostic theist... especially in light of the previous discussion. Despite the fact that I have many questions, and despite my seemingly atheistic criticism of the Old Testament to this point, I must confess that I have no other explanations for the Big Bang and subsequent formation of the universe... than that a God had a hand in it. To my knowledge, there have been no other possibilities put forth by anyone to explain WHY the big bang happened... or how. In light of this fact, I really have no other choice but to accept the ONE possibility that HAS been presented... however preposterous it seems to me. I do, however, reserve the right to change my mind (since that ability was given to me as well). I accept the possibility of God because I can accept it. I reject much of what I have been reading in the Bible because I can reject it. If this attitude is wrong in the eyes of God, the way I see it, it is entirely His own fault for making me the way He did. And if this is blasphemy and I am summarily doomed to Hell for eternity, who will care? Obviously, what I think wouldn't matter...so why would my decisions matter?

January 4, 2013... How To Build A Tent

It is wrenching to me that the revered and widely accepted foundational manuscript of the Christian faith is such an enigma. For two millennia, scholars of merit well beyond mine have pondered its message and meaning... and despite what I consider to be glaringly obvious and ludicrous problems, it is somehow accepted as...well...the gospel. It should be kept in mind here, that I am criticizing the Bible... NOT God. Those who misconstrue my personal study and critical review of it as unfounded atheistic ravings are simply not paying attention.

Throughout most of Genesis and at least the first half of Exodus, a story was told. It is provocative, to be sure, but interesting nonetheless. And although I can find more than a fair amount of questionable pondering points, I acknowledge, with (some) respect, that the story progresses linearly and somewhat logically. And then something odd happens. The continuing adventures of Moses and his people suddenly pauses..and we learn how to make a tent... for many specifically detailed pages and verses. Nearly the entire second half of Exodus is dedicated to the weirdly detailed specifications for building a box, a lamp, a tent, and an altar. And these are not just simple utensils and structures. There is gold... lots of it... and silver, and bronze and jewels, fine weavings, and delicate "artistic" designs.

I realize that the Hebrews plundered Egypt prior to leaving it. They, no doubt, had a number of things that could be used to make the tabernacle and its furnishings, but I cannot help but wonder why God would suddenly be so inordinately specific about how many loops should be on the edge of a portion of a curtain. These people were slaves in Egypt. Although they took plunder with them, they left in haste and traveled on foot. They simply could not have possessed much in the way of belongings that could be taken on a long journey... booty notwithstanding. So, then, if they were poor wanderers in the desert, occasionally lacking in food and water according to the story, why would God specify with such detail and with such authority insist that there be built a glorious tent made from the finest finery? What possible significance might the Lord find in golden accouterments with silver accents and jewels and intricate designs? I can accept that the people might want to build nice things for their chosen deity, but why would the deity Himself dictate that they be so glorious? How do gold and silver play into the salvation of a soul? God, Himself, tells the people not to build golden idols... and then He dictates exactly that for His own bemusement. I acknowledge that an alter is not the same thing as an idol, but they are both used for worship and represent the deity or His greatness.

There is also the matter of the exhaustive list of ordinances given to Moses by God at Si'nai. Without picking away too much, I thought it worthy of mention that there is a considerably detailed account of how to deal with stolen goats and abused slaves and the like. It occurred to me, though, that many of the laws addressed misdeeds that might happen to the people during these times (of three thousand years ago). Did God not foresee a time when time has changed his people and they no longer coveted their neighbor's calf or owned slaves? I can understand how these laws applied to the people at this point in their history, but since they were promised to be "chosen" forever, might they not need a few laws that would be applicable at some later time in their existence? Should they not be wary of coveting their neighbor's WIFI signal? If they should be caught downloading illegal song files, would they not have to repay their trespass with revocation of iPod privileges for a month? Wouldn't hit-and-run victims be entitled to a new Porche?

Obviously, I am being facetious, but my point is this: it seems to me that God was being somewhat short-sighted in promising blessings forever and specifying laws in detail that don't carry well into the future. Are we to assume the responsibility of interpreting the laws to modern times and changing needs? If God thought the people lacked enough in judgment that He felt they needed laws to live by THEN, have we (at least the chosen ones) evolved enough to make the call ourselves now? Everything I have witnessed in my life of sixty years says no. It is my opinion that God may want to make a brief appearance to update a few things.

I am afraid that, again, validity eludes me in Exodus. I simply cannot find any significance to golden furnishings and bejeweled garments... when the point of this whole story concerns the quality and fate of our eternal souls. I have no interest in my neighbor's goat, but I do wonder about my intangible existence and its eventual prospects in the spiritual side of the universe. I do not need to know how to build a fancy tent. I need to know how to detect, repair and nurture my soul...

especially if it exists beyond the lifespan of my physical body. I do not need inter-pretations to live by... I need to find a way to meaningfully "see" the spiritual side of my identity in order to commit to a beneficial path for it to take. Although I have progressed only a short way into the Bible... and fully intend to continue to the end, I am not impressed so far.

January 9, 2013... An Offering of Offerings (Leviticus)

In my earlier days, when I possessed a higher tolerance for the surprising and bla-tant dissemination of blood and gore in books and movies, I might have actually proffered a favorable review of the tedious and detailed killing described in Levit-icus. Had God simply instructed the chosen ones to make an offering of some reasonable sort, I would surely have passed through this "book" with little or no significant concern. It struck me, though, that God, creator of the entire universe... ageless and all-powerful, explicitly requires that perfectly good livestock (not the sick or blemished ones) should be killed and burned as what I see as totally unnec-essary, wasteful, and really quite silly offerings to His greatness. It is quite surpris-ing to me that, as powerful as God is purported to be, He would find any signifi-cance of any degree in the wholesale slaughter, and subsequent burning, of a goat... or in the absence of that... two pigeons.

The strict and absolutely unquestioned performance of these killings is made quite clear... obey or die (as two of Aaron's sons discovered... much to their de-mise). I apologize to any readers who can find sense in this bizarre practice, but in the absence of learned and decisively accurate reasons for it, I proclaim it a savage and ludicrous example of absurdity and ignorance that goes well beyond meaning-ful and purposeful ritual. We have burnt offerings, sin offerings, peace offerings, trespass offerings, and wave offerings. We dip our fingers in blood and touch our right ear, our right thumb, and our right big toe. We sprinkle blood on each other and pour the remainder beside the alter of the tabernacle... which would quickly and noticeably acquire a somewhat unpleasant bouquet I should think. Then we talk about things that are unclean.

And for good measure, I suppose I should mention the uncoverings of family members... which I have to think refers to incest. It really is quite incredible to me that God spells out how taboo incest is... when there are numerous examples of exactly that throughout the previous writings... which goes unnoticed and unpunished. I have not forgotten that despite Leviticus 20:19, Moses' father married his aunt.

January 12, 2013... Vague Needs And Other Uncertainties

During the last several years, I have begun to notice certain feelings that are both disconcerting and mysterious to me. They are difficult to describe... and in fact, elusive enough that I am not wholly sure I can communicate what they are, exactly, or know with any certainty how to deal with them. They are, in large part, one of the reasons I began to look for spirituality of some sort in my life. Years ago, had someone else voiced the same thing, I would have promptly ridiculed him and dismissed him as one of those people who think too much. I have since come to realize that I used to think too little.

I am not a psychologist in any sense of the word, although I remember enough of my college psychology class that I can visualize how my rather dysfunctional upbringing might affect my adult personality and life. I believe that as a protective measure, I suppressed much of my own intangible side. You might say I shut down the spiritual side of me so that the tender young boy simply didn't have to deal with what I came to see as the trouble areas. I replaced most of my psychological turmoil with anger... and later, depression. It took many decades for me to discern what had happened... and to begin to reverse it. This journal is part of that process.

I am afraid I have become what my wife, regretfully, once called "a wimp"... and what I call a "needy" person. I awake most mornings with a distinct and chronic feeling of "not being wanted". It is not pleasant, but there is a message there if I am open to it. I am not "not wanted", therefore, the feeling originates within me... not from someone else's behaviors... or lack of them. For several years, I actually believed that I FELT unwanted because I WASN'T wanted. I was wrong. It was not the "wanted" part that was causing problems; it was the "felt" part. At some point, I belatedly realized that my feelings were suspect. I was actually my own worst enemy... at least when it came to interjecting detrimental and even debilitating thoughts into my otherwise "good" life. Indeed, it was this realization that lead me to begin a search for whatever real and valid, albeit vague and elusive, problems I might have. It is my sincere hope that by opening myself up to the intangible possibilities of spiritual living, I will someday overcome my self-inflicted dysfunctions.

I will admit that I find it most disheartening to know that most of what I find pertaining to spirituality is baseless and nearly completely speculative. So far, every source of information... including the Bible... makes claims that have no basis in truth... at least no scientifically valid truth. The Bible, in particular, uses itself as the basis for its validity... which I find totally preposterous. Likewise, nearly every other spiritual source I have come upon makes groundless claims and bases recommended actions on interpretations and personal opinions. It is quite disappointing to finally see how important our spiritual side likely is, only to find nothing of universal validity or benefit to support the many claims. Can it really be that a very real and absolutely essential part of every human being is undetectable, immeasurable, unreachable, and arguably unfixable? Somehow, we are able to affect our spiritual side by introducing dysfunction into our lives... can we not also introduce non-dysfunctional, beneficial actions that positively... and permanently... improve our intangible existence? Is it possible to administer these positive actions without the usual guesswork? There are more than enough "valid studies" to show that yoga, meditation, acupuncture, or a Christian leap of faith can do wonders for us, but it appears to me that, although there is almost certainly SOME legitimacy to these practices, none of them seem to jump out at me as a real and proven activity that will make a measurable difference. I will, however, be quite happy to be shown that I am wrong (take a number, though).

January 13, 2013... To Think A Truth, Or Not To Think A Truth

I have been thinking, today... about thinking. Earlier, I touched on consciousness, intangible existence and identity, with little progress toward any valid explanation of any of it, but it occurred to me, today, that the very fact that I think... validates the parallel existence of my own spirit. This assumes MY definition of spirit as the intangible side of physical existence. We all probably think primarily of HUMAN existence when we consider our spirit or soul, but I will not limit my possibilities in that regard at this point... though, for discussion ease, I will limit my thoughts to MY spirit for the most part.

Perhaps I should digress a bit and first ask myself if I do, indeed, think. I certainly think that I think. What, exactly, is thinking? Although it would seem prudent to "look it up", I will explore this on my own...I think. There is obviously something going on in my brain that results in electrical pulses stimulating neural centers with the eventual, although nearly instant, production of ideas. These thoughts are peculiar in that we don't seem to have a very good idea of what they are, how they came to exist (if they really do), or why. Theists will likely attribute their origin and validity to God. Atheists, however, do not have this option available to them... and will probably find themselves deferring to some future brilliant discovery. Where does this leave me? As a self-declared agnostic theist, I am willing to acknowledge the existence of a God, but I really find it fairly ludicrous that a being (or whatever) that great could have any interest whatsoever in whether I think or not. I, therefore, lean at this point toward some sort of evolutionary happenstance whereby the physical brain, somehow manages to "connect" to an intangible and undetectable part of the universe... perhaps dark energy... and interacts with it for a brief moment in time (our lifetime). This will almost certainly sound incredible and laughable to many, but I am looking at possibilities here, not facts. I think it would be very difficult for anyone of acknowledged brilliance to discount my possibility as false when there is no more to base that judgment on than I have in my original hypothesis. I am quite sure that I am not the only one to have expounded a preposterous idea only for it to become a proven fact at some later time. Remember the earth was the center of the universe until Copernicus came along... although previous societies suspected otherwise.

So for now, I think. And since the substance of thinking is plainly not based in the physical world... at least the known physical world... it can be safely assumed in our ignorance that thoughts reside in an unknown part of the universe that I will refer to as the intangible reality. This will sound like an obvious oxymoron, but if we all acknowledge that we think and feel and have a spiritual identity, and if we can agree that these things are not tangible, and if we believe they are "real", then an intangible reality exists... or at least we can say that we think so.

Like thoughts, themselves, truth is an elusive prospect. Our arrogance allows us to make up our own rules about everything whether based on facts or whimsy or something in between. And there are a great many people in the world... each one with independent thoughts. Occasionally, a group of people will form a consensus about a thought and declare it the truth. Conveniently, when people of merit proffer ideas, those ideas are often accepted and built upon and fought over and sanctified and archived for future generations to drool over. Sometimes, though, they are proven or disproven... and it falls to the faithful to attempt to discredit the proof... which really is an oxymoron. It amazes me that, even in these supposedly enlightened times, people will simply discount proofs in the interests of defending a belief. An example would be the issue of global warming. An overwhelming majority of scientists the world over have accumulated factual information with scientific proof that undeniably implicates the actions of humans in the warming of our planet... with eventual consequences pointing toward a seriously and negatively impacted human condition. Would I really find it worthwhile to dispute these proven findings simply because I don't want to believe it? No... but many do. Incredible. Truth matters, but only if it is seen as real. The key word here is "seen". What we see is not always what is there. And strangely enough, this is also what validates the doubters; if they don't "see" the proofs as they are, then they are "seen" as they aren't. Hence, truth is in question... despite the fact that it shouldn't be. Truth, then, becomes a matter of what we think rather than what is true. I hate it when that happens.

January 14, 2013... The Origin of the Census Bureau (Numbers)

I have only progressed a very short way into the book of Numbers at this point, but a few questions come to mind that will not go away. These questions might all be summed up with one word: why? God instructed Moses to take a census of his people... and in particular, those of a male persuasion and of an age to be of use in war. Here, then, is another burst of what many might consider tedious and frustratingly stupid questions... however meaningful they may appear to me: Shouldn't God have already known how many people there were? Is He not all-knowing? If He did already know, was it His intention to let Moses know how many there were? Why would it matter? If God was planning an invasion, and with all the power that supposedly was at His disposal, why would it matter how many invaders invaded? Was it not God's will that the invaded would be defeated regardless? Why did God need an army in the first place? Were there no other seas to part? What about a nice, nasty, sizeable sandstorm? ...or maybe another dose of pestilence? ...or even a simple click of the fingers? Please excuse my blasphemy, but if I was a god, with an eye on providing a place for my "chosen" people, I would just create it with the snap of my fingers. I would not sacrifice a substantial number of the very people I desire to help when I am quite capable of finding or creating a homeland for them in other ways. And hypothetically, if I did have that kind of power, why would I create a (non-chosen) people who seem to be in the way of my own plans... and then have to eliminate them in a bloody and totally unnecessary manner?

If I understand what is happening so far in the Old Testament... and I am quite sure I will be assured that I don't, God appears to do things inconsistently, with no apparent discernable reason, and with a very questionable disregard for His own previous workings. Although, as I also understand it, He moves in mysterious ways. How very convenient.

When the time comes for the rather large group to begin their trek through the wilderness, it is proclaimed that God will act as navigator... lowering Himself in the form of a dark cloud, by day, onto the place where an encampment is to be made, with a final resting place hovering over the tabernacle of meeting. By night, the cloud becomes fiery so as to be seen by the people. If the cloud should rise, the people are to strike camp and follow it. If the cloud descends, pitch camp. If someone among the chosen ones gets sick and begins to have a discharge of some sort, they are to be thrown out of camp and shunned. If someone touches any holy object, he dies. If the holy things are being transported to the next campsite, they are to be covered with badger skins. If someone complains, he dies. If a man becomes jealous of his wife... even if she has done nothing... she must atone at the alter. If someone happens to be near a person who dies, he is unclean and must present a sin offering and a burnt offering. Mysterious ways or not, this all smacks of just plain silliness.

January 20, 2013... The Appearance of Historical Account

It has not been lost on me that, although mere humans are probably capable of creating a rather exhaustive and convincing fictional account of historical events, there have been many novels written that were based on a true story. Who am I to decide, in my historical ignorance, whether the story put forth in the Old Testament is true, based on truth, or wholly fictitious? I freely admit to a well-earned antiknowledge... complete with many holes representing what I do not know and do not understand. Regardless, though, I don't believe I can be totally dismissed as undeniably stupid or hopelessly unteachable. I am discussing all of this with myself for the very purpose of learning as I go. Whether I actually accomplish my hoped-for result of spiritual validity or not remains to be seen.

If Numbers is anything, it is a historical account of the wanderings of the people of Israel... or at least some of it. I can't help but think that learned theologians might interpret circles around me as I struggle with my questions and observations. I also believe, however, that even in my ignorance, I could probably give the most confident Old Testament advocate a frustrating challenge when it comes to the indiscriminate use of interpretation. Until someone spells out to me in no uncertain terms exactly what the rules of interpretation are, and why, and who says so, and what gives them the authority to say so, I will stand on my own thoughts and establish my own opinions as to the validity of what I read.

The wanderings of the chosen people are all well and good; ridiculous, but palatable. My most pressing question, as stated earlier, is simply why(?). I can understand why the people of Israel repeatedly angered the Lord with their incessant complaints and never-ending transgressions. They obviously wondered at just exactly HOW chosen they were... when they were led around the desert for 40 years after being promised the promised land-based NOT on THEIR behaviors, but on the previous behaviors of Abraham, Isaac, Jacob, and Moses. Their constant stream of frustrations in attaining their goal was repeatedly hindered by their actions, but the promised land was very much still promised. Moses even found himself interceding on behalf of the congregation more than once when God was about to change His mind and call the whole thing off. Why wasn't Moses put to death for questioning the wrath of God? When the people questioned their circumstances, God killed 27,000 of them. When the army of Israel defeated the Mid'i-an-ites, the captive women and children were taken to Moses who commanded the army to kill all the non-virgin women and all the male children... the rest to be slaves. Again, why would God create a nation of people who would stand in the way of his own plans... and then command a war to deal with them? How many of the Israelites died in battle because God frustrated His own plans? Am I to accept that God DIDN'T create the Mid'i-an-ites or allow them to be in the way of the exodus? Is it to be understood that God only created SOME people and not others? Did He only have jurisdiction over CERTAIN people and not others? Where might these others have come from, then? If God created the earth, and we obviously are meant to believe He did, were not the Mid'i-an-ites of the earth? If God didn't create the Mid'i-an-ites, who did? If He DID, then why would He be angry with them for being there... when He, Himself, put them there? Why would He need a war to deal with them? Why would He sacrifice some of His precious chosen people to defeat them? Why was it necessary to briefly have a talking donkey?

Thinking about it, I confess a certain amount of validity to the appearance of a historical chronology. It can't be denied that a considerable amount of detail has been set down for posterity in the Old Testament... accurate or not. One cannot dismiss the likelihood that much of it is a real accounting of real events that transpired around a certain time in real history. There is also the likelihood that much of what is described is validated by other historical documents of the time or compelling evidence that, at least, points to actual events. I really don't dispute the general story of it all... only what appears to me as senseless, preposterous, or unsubstantiated and interpreted embellishments... which reside, I admit, in the realm of what I find questionable. Others may find my findings worthy of little consideration for whatever reasons. I respect that in others, whether I agree or not... on the condition that I am accorded the same courtesy.

February 3, 2013... Honesty and Faith

An idea came to me today... about the difference between the honesty of thought and the diligence of faith. The title of this day's discussion nearly read, "Honesty VS Faith", but I realized, in the nick of time, that I might easily pit two ideas against one another that do not necessarily need to be at odds. They are not, in fact, mutually exclusive... or opposites, but they are both choices... at least as I see them. Not being of a particularly philosophical bent, I have not, in truth, given either idea the due they deserve... however much I desire it now. My discussion of them here and now will be brief, and no doubt lacking, but my intentions are honorable enough... to glean out a small measure of understanding with which to further my quest for that elusive and mysterious part of human existence I call spirituality... for lack of a better term. I actually prefer to refer to my spirituality as my intangible existence... but I would rather say one word than two.

What, exactly, is honesty? One dictionary defined it as the quality of being truthful. Well, assuming that truthfulness is the expression of truth, what, then, is truth? The same dictionary says, with comfortable authority, that truth is a proven fact. What then, is proof? Once again, the same dictionary says, "evidence that forces belief". This might easily go on. I think, though, that I can safely say that honesty happens when an undeniable proof supports a given truth, though I wonder (in all honesty) if it might be more. One might say, for instance, that I am being honest if I make an earnest attempt to express my heartfelt beliefs. In this instance, I might be considered honest for baring my genuine thoughts... even though those same thoughts might actually not represent true or proven ideas. A question arises, then... can a person honestly express a belief that isn't actually factual? The answer, of course, is yes. Honestly expressing a belief is an honest action, whereas the stated belief may or may not be a factual idea. So being honest is not necessarily the same thing as expressing a truth.

What about faith? The dictionary says it is a belief that does not require proof to substantiate it. If ever there was a most convenient and thoroughly unarguable idea, this is it. What better contrivance of man can there be than one that allows any idea, by any person, to be completely convincing, without evidence to support it, and which is expected to be thoroughly accepted, defended, and disseminated to all with no regard whatsoever for proof or truth? I will be careful not to swear, here, that anyone who attempts to inflict this kind of thinking on me will most certainly find himself confronted by my questions regarding honesty and motive. Although I freely admit to a decided, and long-practiced, lack of faith in my life, I cannot simply accept unsubstantiated ideas... however well-founded they may be... simply on the basis of overwhelming acceptance by others. Human beings have demonstrated many times throughout history that they are more than capable, en masse, to practice abhorrent beliefs with the denigration and butchery of millions to illustrate the point. So, when a person says to me that I should accept Christianity, for instance, because millions of people around the world can't be wrong, I say they most certainly CAN be wrong, HAVE been wrong, and likely ARE wrong now. But I am also not above admitting that I, likewise, can also be wrong.

Is it possible, then, to have faith... and also be honest? "Thou shalt not bear false witness..." It seems to depend, somewhat, on who is honest with whom. If, for instance, I lie to you, my deceit will likely be seen as dishonesty. If, though, I deceive myself, there is a question of ignorance that comes into play. If I convince myself (through choice or brainwashing) that a deity created me to have faults... and therefore lie, then is it not correct for me to behave as I was designed? Would I be lying to say, "God made me do it."? I can certainly believe that God exists... and that He created me in His image, faults and all, but can I say that He made a mistake when He created me with the capability to lie? What point is made when God creates a man who isn't perfect, and who makes mistakes, and then condemns him for doing what he was created to do? If I am honest with myself, can I not ask questions that are uncomfortable for others... if I am genuinely interested in how they are resolved? If I am on a heartfelt and genuine quest for the validity of spirituality, can I not be seen as behaving in an honest way? Are my honest actions somehow an affront to those who don't happen to share my God-given apprehensions? It appears to me that the conflicts that happen all too often are the result of the misunderstandings of faith... not a matter of truths. I have a real problem with blind faith... and let's be honest here; since faith is not based on proofs, it is all too convenient to simply ignore truths in the interests of faith. I do not wish to offend others with this statement, but I, for one, prefer to put truths and evidence before faith-based reasoning. If God, in His infinite wisdom, created me to be exactly the way I am... in the interest of His mysterious ways, then I cannot be denigrated by my honest and sincere manifestation of His own plan for me. I have no doubts, however, that someone likely will attempt exactly that.

February 6, 2013... Lest Ye Forget

It is interesting, in Deuteronomy, that Moses finds it necessary to review the prior adventures of God and His people in speeches detailing all the highlights of the last forty years or so. The chronology is almost certainly meant to remind those who might have survived the exodus how important and necessary and crucial the exodus and its subsequent wilderness wanderings were to the inevitable inheritance of the promised land. It also served to state, in no uncertain terms and for the benefit of the newer generations, that even after 40 years of what seems to me to be pointless wandering, God isn't messing around. All the chosen people, new or otherwise, absolutely must appreciate the power, glory, and the covenant of God...or else.

What is also interesting... to me, at least, is that the NON-chosen people do not seem to have much significance to God. He routinely commands the Israelites to kill men, women, and children to the last. If I understand things correctly, God created the earth and everything on it... but apparently felt the need for some disposable people of no particular worth to get in the way of His own plans for His chosen ones. It is disconcerting to me that a (THE) deity with the power He claims to possess should repeatedly put unimportant and worthless living beings in the way as impediments to His own plan for those He favors. I freely admit my ignorance with respect to His "mysterious ways", but this entire scenario appears more than a little ridiculous to me.

All in all, I will confess a certain acceptance of Deuteronomy. Unlike a good part of the previous books of the Bible, this one does not put forth any new and wild stories which in any other book would be promptly and decisively ridiculed as unfounded, improbable, and unexplainable. It does, however, review what has already been stated... as if that will validate it. Although others may disagree with me, I cannot accept that repetition of a story validates it. The line-by-line reiteration of God's rules for the chosen ones is plain enough. I have questions, to be sure, but generally, I can concede that a clarifying review of God's commandments and laws does no harm.

There is one rather strange idea that I will mention. God commands (through Moses) that in each of the inherited areas of the promised land, three cities be designated as "safe zones" where perpetrators of accidental killings can go and be exempt from the revenge of their unintended victim's revengers. If I remember correctly, there are twelve families... and therefore twelve inheritance zones... each one with three cities designated safe zones. My math notwithstanding, it seems quite odd that around thirty-six cities would be needed for these accidental killers to find refuge in. I might ask how many accidental killings did the chosen people have in those days? Who decided as to whether a killing was accidental or not? ...the killer? If not the killer, who then? ...the victim's survivors? ...an accidental killing committee? ...a designated accidental killing judge? If an accidental killer fled to one of the many refuge cities, how then was the killer protected from the revengers within the safe zone? ...good faith self-service? If an angry survivor was angry enough to want revenge, and be willing to kill to get it, would the city limits, alone, be enough to dissuade him from his self-appointed task? ...or would there be an accidental killer protection committee? ...or perhaps all of the inhabitants of the entire city would take it upon themselves to blockade attempts from revengers to gain entrance? This is assuming that the revenger identified himself as an avenger upon approach to the safe zone. I wonder, though, if a potential avenger might actually lower himself to the dastardly level of hiding his intentions so as to gain entrance into the safe city to find his revengee. I should think it would be on the head of the city gate screener to see through and prevent these unlikely scenarios. I would not want that job.

Oh, and one other thing... What if an accidental killer... in a designated safe zone... with sword in hand... was found to have accidentally cut his own head off? Case closed?

At the end of Deuteronomy, we encounter the end of Moses. Although being one of the five books of Moses, Deuteronomy is written in the third person. As I understand it, the first five books of the Bible are the inspired word of God as written by Moses. Why then, did Moses write of himself in the third person... as a character in some other story rather than of himself in his own story. Allowing for artistic license, I can accept that Moses might do that. Perhaps some convention I am ignorant of makes this an accepted practice... at least in this particular work. How, though, does he briefly describe his own death and burial somewhere in a nearby, but undisclosed, valley? According to his own words, Moses went up onto the mountain where he was able to see the promised land... despite not being allowed to actually go there. I assume that he was able to document that occurrence since he was not, at that particular time, deceased, but then he did die... or so he writes. He was then buried in the nearby valley. Who exactly witnessed these things and documented them? No one was with Moses when he died or was buried. Who wrote the last few lines of Deuteronomy? ...Samwise Gamgee?

February 12, 2013... Brief Overview of the Pentateuch

It should be quite unabashedly clear by now how impressed I am with what I know of the Bible so far. I believe I have probably set forth most of the misgivings that, no doubt, have been argued by others of more learned credentials for centuries... and, therefore, have likely surprised few who understand what the word agnostic means. Although I am certainly not a Bible expert by any sad stretch of the imagination, I do possess the mental and literary wherewithal to, at the very least, express in my own way what I truly think. With my honesty and willingness to share my views, there is a risk I could easily offend those who don't happen to agree with my observations or interpretations. I will reiterate that my purpose here is to discuss my thoughts with myself... but open my musings to anyone who is willing to form their own opinions without serious regard for mine.

For what it is worth, I proclaim the books of Moses to be simply "based on a true story". I have no particular qualification to make that claim, but I have as much right to my opinions as anyone. It will take a very wise, unconfrontational, and patient proponent of its authenticity to convince me otherwise. I admit to an ignorance of the history of the times and location of its occurrences. I concede a bias toward proofs and away from faith. If I am expected to accept the physical occurrence of miracles, I expect to see physical proof of them. For the sake of those who would find fault in my thinking, I also accept that contrary opinions are as valid as mine.

I wonder about the motive for the overall story in the Pentateuch. One possibility is that the story is true and God "inspired" Moses to write it... miracles and all. Another is that a curious combination of ingredients such as imagination and the passage of time... mingled their respective flavors to produce a soup of a story that is "based on a true story". Still, another is that the chosen people (the Jews) found themselves looked down upon after the Jesus fiasco and contrived a written account of their existence that serves to redeem them. One thing about possibilities...there is no limit to them... though I must bear in mind that thinking one up does not validate it.

Without having read further than Deuteronomy, I have only my previous vague remembrances to tell me that the next several books detail the continuing adventures of the chosen ones as they savagely conquer the various inconsequential peoples who God created to get in the way of His own plans for the Hebrews. Despite my apparently negative and all-too-biased reactions to my readings, I truly am willing to discover and accept valid reasons to become a "believer". I sincerely hope these reasons are forthcoming.

February 13, 2013... An Interlude of Intangibleness

This day weighs heavy on me. I wrestle with altogether too familiar feelings of lostness and the weary weight of past pain and the present results of it. Some would call it a depression of sorts; I don't really. I see it not so much as a chemical imbalance in the brain... though it likely is, as a very real, albeit intangible, feeling that has a cause and an effect. I absolutely know what bothers me... though I will not go into it here, but I am unable to affect a change. This inability is the disconcerting reason my affliction lingers. It occurs to me that I have a feeling that affects me physically and emotionally. I can show no proof of it... it is intangible. How then can I expect others to know that I have this feeling, and that it affects me to the very real degree it does, with no way, other than expressing it vocally (or writing it here), to prove it? I have little doubt that since others can relate to feelings like this, they can readily accept that I have them. We all have feelings; do we not?

Where am I going with this? Essentially, the acceptance of my feelings, as viewed by others, is a matter of faith. I cannot prove that I am feeling low. Others will just have to believe me when I say it is true. Is it possible, then, that I, myself, am a living example of how faith works? The game is not over, but it seems I may have scored a point for the other team. Did I not say I was feeling lost?

February 14, 2013... The Sorcerer's Apprentice (Joshua)

It is probably an unwritten rule in the book of fate that whosoever works a wonder first is seen as the great perpetrator of wonders. Moses, then, gets the glory in that he parted the Red Sea to let his people flee from the doomed Egyptian pursuers. Then Joshua takes up the challenge and parts the river Jordan allowing the chosen ones a dry crossing over to the gates of Jericho and the promised land. This is no less a feat, but somehow doesn't go through history as the great and remembered miracle it should have. Perhaps if an army suffered a great drowning as in the Red Sea, we of latter generations would be more properly impressed. As it is, we are relegated to remember the great sorcery with a pile of rocks designated for this purpose by God, Himself.

God, for His part, is not idle during this time. He meanwhile devises the perfect solution to the problem of Jericho's high city walls... a barrier of some significance for the invading marauders, I mean...the chosen people of God. Joshua is to huff and puff, and...oh, that's another story. Joshua is to march once around the city each day for six days while blowing the horns... and then seven times on the seventh day with a big shout afterwards. What city of considerable fortification could withstand an onslaught like that? Down came the walls and the maraud...I mean, chosen people of God waltzed in and slaughtered every man, woman, child, donkey, and goat in the place... except for the harlot, whose sanctioned lies protected Joshua's spies from being captured. This inspiring story is sure to strike wonder and awe into the hearts of all who hear it... or read it. I, however, will allow my satirical retelling of it to speak for itself. One small note of observation: Isn't there supposed to be a Sabbath in there somewhere... according to the un-negotiable covenant of God?

I also noted, with my typical and invariable surprise, that after the defeat and razing of Jericho, Joshua built an alter nearby with the stones from the Jordan as commanded by God. He then, again, according to the commandment of God, offered peace offerings on it. PEACE offerings! This immediately before invading the entire area, totally slaughtering everyone, and "utterly destroying" everything in the entire "promised" land... except the "booty", of course. I, personally, would find myself consulting the nearest available dictionary regarding the apparently variable definition of peace.

February 18, 2013... Judges and Grudges

It is stated in Judges that after the death of Joshua a few peoples were "left" to "test" the people of Israel. Although I have voiced (written) my wonderment already concerning the reasons why God would bother testing the people that He, himself, chose for favored status, I find it difficult, indeed, to grasp what the Old Testament is actually about. A member of the chosen ones has written an account of being chosen by God... and then strangely encounters frustration after frustration... both for the chosen ones and for God, Himself. I'm afraid that I cannot help wondering why God might find it worthwhile to choose a people who He favors at all, much less one that needs to be tested repeatedly when He often cites, in advance, that they will fail Him over and over. When the people sin in the face of the Lord, He reacts with anger and wrath. Why? He already knew they would fail. He actually CAUSED them to fail by putting people in their way that would frustrate them or lead them astray. Then, He punished them when they actually did what He meant for them to do. I am likely misinterpreting something here, but then that nagging interpretation question arises again. Am I not meant to understand this book or not?

February 19, 2013... Abominations

I have encountered a passage in Judges that I hadn't heard about previously, and which strikes me as rather strange and perplexing. It takes place after six concurrent episodes of the chosen people transgressing the covenant of God... and accordingly suffering His wrath time after time. It is described in Judges 11:30—39 and involves Jeph'thah... who makes a "covenant" of his own with God by promising to offer a burnt offering of the first thing that runs out of his door if God will allow him to defeat the people of Am'mon in battle. God lives up to His part of the bargain by delivering the children of Am'mon to his hand and they are summarily defeated. When Jeph'thah returns home, the first thing that runs out of his door is his only daughter Miz'peh, who he then kills (after two months) and offers as a burnt offering to God as promised... thereby fulfilling his part of the bargain. Now I am not, by any means, an expert in these matters, but I am reasonably certain that this passage describes a sanctioned human sacrifice by one of the favored ones... according to an agreement with God, and with His full knowledge. I have no doubts that what seems plain enough to me will be interpreted to death by others... and likely dismissed somehow or discounted as the literary interloping of someone's imagination. Assuming my own interpretations are as valid as anyone else's, I am obliged to declare this an obvious example of God violating His own rules. The inspired word of God clearly describes an agreement made between a man and God involving human sacrifice... which, unless my memory tricks me, was earlier prohibited as an abomination. Without investigating what is likely a somewhat hot topic of debate on the internet, I can see this as nothing else.

I am quite aware that the Bible is an assembled work of literature... although touted to be the inspired word of God. As such, it must necessarily suffer from the various differences inherent in both, the writers of it and the readers of it. I could understand how parts of the Bible might be discounted or explained away if a disclaimer were included that referenced the inevitable failings of the human contributors of it, but there is no such disclaimer. By my understanding, the book, in fact, is purported to be the inspired word of God... a sacred and deity-inspired history and handbook for living. If the Bible is, indeed, meant for the masses to use as a guide for spiritual living, then as one of those masses, I find fault with it.

I accept the condemnation from others as an inevitable response to this state-ment... as the opinions of others are no less valid than my own, but I also insist on the respect of my opinions for the very same reason.

Then there is Samson, who was "judge" for twenty years for the chosen ones. Strength or no strength, he is described as having killed one thousand armed war-riors with the jawbone of a donkey. Am I seriously to regard this as one of God's miracles? I defy anyone to make sense of this. He also obviously suspects De-li'lah of treachery since he lies to her three times about the source of his strength. Despite her treachery (three times), he still eventually tells her the "secret" of his hair and he is captured and blinded. I find it more than a little difficult to accept that the chosen leader of the Children of Israel is stupid enough to divulge his weakness to a proven advocate for his enemies. It is true that this all eventually led to the down-fall of the Philistines' leaders and temple, but with his obvious, God-given, strength (and apparent arrogance), could he not have simply zipped over there and wielded his jawbone at them (with the backing of the Lord, of course)? I am no Hemingway (or Moses for that matter), but I believe I could have come up with a better true story than that.

February 23, 2013... A Friend Indeed is a Friend in Need

In these last few recent days, I have been thinking about the curious state of psy-chological need... as it applies to me and others. This came about as I was experi-encing one of my occasional bouts of moodiness, for which I am known, alas. It occurred to me that my moodiness, which was always simply "the way things are" and quite normal for me, was actually a manifestation of psychological need. One of my initial questions to myself was whether or not this feeling really was a need... or actually a want. I decided on the former... primarily due to the fact that I nearly always feel that what I don't have is something I can't have. That is, whatever my desire is, I am not able, for whatever reason, to attain it on my own. There may be people who believe that everything is within our power to achieve or attain... I'm not one of them. Although we humans are amazingly resourceful... and we can make many unlikely things happen, we cannot, for instance, make someone love us. We can't simply wish our bills away... although we can earn them away.

Need, though, is intriguing, as well as somewhat disconcerting, as it relates to our intangible existence. Need is a feeling. Feelings are intangible manifestations of the mind. The mind is the intangible product of the brain. The intrigue of need is disconcerting when the fulfilling of the need is beyond the capability of the needy. Thus, in my case, moodiness results. I know that this is the case... and I know what my need is, but when it is beyond my capability to realize, I feel dejected and unfulfilled. Where is all of this going?

It occurred to me that since need is an intangible feeling, perhaps spirituality is at least one way of dealing with it. I am groping in the dark here... bear with me. To say that spirituality might be of help to one in need is to make a claim that I cannot substantiate, but it seems to me that this is one of the principal reasons for spirituality in the first place... or so it is inferred. I offer myself up for scrutiny on this topic. So here is my question: If I have a need... and I seek spirituality to find comfort, will spirituality suffice? ...or do I still, at some point, need my need to be fulfilled? In this case, is spirituality a band-aid? ...or a real fix? There are probably no easy answers. What kind of spirituality? What is the need? How possible is the attainment of it? Can the need be distracted away? ...or minimized? ...or eliminated entirely?

If I were to accept God... I mean, REALLY accept Him, would my own needs become so insignificant that they essentially aren't needs anymore? If I were to pray for relief... in earnest, should I expect that relief will come? What should I expect with spirituality? Surely if I decide to accept a form of spirituality, I should expect that something will come of it. Will I feel comforted? Will I find that a measure of positive thinking is required, as well? ...in this case, did the spirituality work, or did the positive thinking work? Is it possible that spirituality is nothing more than organized positive thinking? Is there really something called mind over matter?

Lots of questions, to be sure, but they come, you know. What, exactly, is spirituality? One dictionary described it as a connection to God or a spirit world. I tend to think that spirituality isn't so much a connection as much as an intangible

way of life. I would call prayer... and maybe meditation... connections to spirituality. Unfortunately, these are all subjective... both the questions and the possible
answers. I hate it when that happens.

February 24, 2013... Nearly Ruthless

Except for the mention of generations leading to the birth of David, the Book of
Ruth is as uneventful as it is short. It may be refreshing to any reader of this journal
that I find no problems of significance in it to pick apart... and no reason to "discuss" it further.

February 26, 2013... The Rise and Fall of Saul (Samuel)

The first book of Samuel, although somewhat confusing because I am not familiar
with many of the family names and places mentioned, very nearly struck me as
having no seriously questionable passages for me to take issue with... until I encountered the story of Saul. And compared to some of my previous concerns, the
Saul problems are perhaps less troublesome.

If I understand things correctly, God selected Saul to be king over the Israelites
as a spite, of sorts... in answer to their sin of dissatisfaction with God's rule over
them. The people saw that other peoples had a king to lead them and so decided
it would be a good thing for them, as well. Prior to this, as I see it, the chosen ones
were led by their prophets and judges. I suppose one could say that there was a
transition from a theocracy to a monarchy. God had declared several times, previously, that He was a jealous God... He, therefore, took offense to the desire of the
chosen ones to have a political leader. He Himself, however, chose Saul... and later
when Saul didn't work out so well, He "repented" that He had chosen him as king
(1-Samuel 15:35). It seems odd to me that God could repent anything. Did He
not cause the very thing that disappointed Him? Once more, it appears that God
made a mistake, acknowledged it, and then took steps to rectify it. Is this not another case of trial and error on God's part?

On a related note and a bit later, God instructs Samuel to inspect the sons of
Jesse whereupon one would be pointed out to be a replacement king for Saul.

Samuel then, one-by-one, looks them over and thinks he sees suitable candidates until God tells him that he only looks at the outward appearances... whereas He (God) sees into the heart. David is thus chosen. It occurred to me, though, that if God has the ability to look into a person's heart, He should have seen that Saul's disobedience was merely an effort, on his part, to glorify God by not slaughtering all the Am'a-lek-ite's sheep and holding a few back to offer as a sacrifice. Saul's sin was one of good heart... despite the fact that it was disobedience in a minor way. He did, after all, slaughter all the men, women, children, and nearly all of the animals... as instructed.

It appears to me, then, that God (in spite) chose Saul as king over the chosen ones, acknowledged it was a mistake and repented doing it, then thought of a lame excuse to replace Saul, and finally, in His mysterious way, pointed out David as a suitable replacement. It has been made reasonably clear that God did not like the idea of the Hebrew's wish to have a king in the first place... but He gave them one anyway. When it didn't work out, He gave them another one.

I don't understand why God would play cat and mouse with Saul and David, though. He was plainly disappointed with Saul... and He was plainly pleased with David. But instead of simply killing Saul off, as He did with Na'bal, God repeatedly inflicted Saul with a bad spirit and temporary madness. If He wanted to make Saul suffer for a time, He also made David suffer because of it. This seems to be a rather poor and unnecessary plan for the rise of King David.

February 27, 2013... A Brief Thought Regarding Mythology

In all honesty, I am not entirely sure where I am about to go with the idea that just occurred to me. As a sideline distraction, I am currently reading Gore Vidal's Creation... a historical novel involving the Persian Empire and its aspirations for eastward expansion into India and Cathay. With a title like Creation, my curiosity was piqued and so I began reading with the vague expectation that I might encounter ideas of relevance to discuss here in my spirituality quest. So far, two thirds finished with this wonderful book... that is not the case. I did, however, notice a curious similarity in the way the Greek Gods were perceived to "play" with humans on earth... and the tests that God occasionally inflicted on His chosen ones. I find myself wondering about the all too human accounts... written by people... about Gods who, for some elusive reason, feel the need to "mess with" the people they wish to preside over. I wonder why people believe (or believed) this was something their Gods would do. I wonder why a God would ever consider what seems to me to be a completely unnecessary and really quite silly action on their part. Why are people tested when they are supposedly created to be inherently fallible? Why would a God care in the least if the very imperfect people He created didn't behave perfectly? Why would anything people do be of concern to a God in the first place? How could people be of any concern whatsoever to a timeless, omnipotent, omniscient God who is capable of creating or eliminating a universe with a snap of the divine fingers? I wonder if at some point in the future people will look back at the Christian era (...or Buddhist, or Shinto, or whatever) and see it as just another time of ignorance and mythology. The ancient Greeks believed their gods were real... so do modern Christians. The ancient Romans believed their gods tested their people... so do modern Christians. The ancient Egyptians believed their gods were all-powerful and timeless... so do modern Christians. The ancient Norse people believed that they would ascend to a heaven of sorts (Valhalla)... so do modern Christians. Is it possible that this entire God idea is simply one of our many human idiosyncrasies? Can I be faulted for wondering?

February 28, 2013... Stepping Back For Another Look

Although I can find little of major significance in the books of Samuel to question or criticize, I do have one small point of curiosity. Although the first book of Samuel concerns the life of the prophet Samuel, it also concerns the life of Saul. Whether the book is called Samuel or Saul is of no real import in my eyes, but the second book of Samuel details historical events that took place after the death of Samuel... and Saul. It describes the rise and reign of David... and is a fascinating, if not tumultuous, story. It would seem sensible for the second book, then, to be called the book of David... but then I am fairly certain that biblical historians have their reasons for doing what they do... me notwithstanding.

Although my journey through the Old Testament might likely be seen as tedious and disturbing for certain others, I should point out that I fully expect the New Testament to have considerable redeeming value. I do not, however, wish to forget that I am open to any other valid spiritual possibilities that I may encounter as I trudge through the Bible. If I was really as conscientious in my quest as I sometimes try to appear, I might find it necessary to include in my investigations the writings of Buddha or Muhammad, Hinduism, or others. If I was to do that, though, I would have to think about considerably more than I find palatable or desirable... and write the largest book ever written. As sincere as I am about all of this, I am not that conscientious.

I wonder, though, if the human imagination and the limits of human capabilities might possibly be leading all of us in entirely wrong directions. It has been demonstrated many times in the past that we don't always know what we don't know. The earth turned out NOT to be the center of the universe... despite the fact that the Christian church made it abundantly clear that it most certainly was... on pain of death. Likewise, neither was the sun. Galaxies didn't exist until relatively recently. Radio waves, without the science behind them, would have been magic. I doubt anyone would seriously tout the continued existence of Zeus and Thor. Would I be ostracized as a troublesome heretic for wondering about the possibilities of other possibilities?

I have made mention of one possible explanation for our intangible existence previously... the idea of our "spirits" residing in another dimension. I wonder now, though, if there could be other possibilities that haven't been thought of at all... or at least given rational consideration. The mystery of creation aside, what exactly is our intangible existence? Where exactly does it come from and where does it truly reside? Where does it go when we die... if it goes anywhere? If we do, indeed, have a spiritual side, why do we have it in the first place? There are probably endless questions regarding this, and it is only that I recognize my own limited capability to understand such things that I acknowledge the possibility of a God deity. When other choices are as limited as they are elusive, it seems natural enough to choose one possibility over another based on not much more than the wide acceptance of it. How can perhaps a billion or two people be wrong to believe in the Christian God? Who am I to question two thousand years of dogma?

Without talk of alien origins or the wrestlings of various deities, I think it might be worthwhile to stretch a bit and see if other possibilities are as wild and unlikely as parts of the Old Testament seem to be to me. One idea might be related to the four fundamental forces of nature... which, most assuredly, were not known at all a few hundred years ago... a short time considering the 13.8 billion year life of the universe. The four forces are gravity, electromagnetic radiation, the weak and the strong nuclear forces. What if there are others that have not been discovered yet... ones that we don't have the ability to detect as yet? Might there be a "force" of thoughts and feelings that our brains somehow are able to link with in some unfathomable way? I realize that wild speculation serves little purpose, but all discoveries stem from either accidental findings or pursued ideas. My ideas might very well be as valid and possible as any others that were at one time only theories or dreams. What harm is there in opening up to possibilities when it is the manifestation of right and wrong that eventually builds into a knowledge of truth?

I certainly recognize my intangible existence. I don't know how, exactly, but I do... and I think everyone else acknowledges theirs, as well. Somehow, we are able to agree that we all exist on a spiritual level that is, as yet, unprovable. We say, in fact, that it is a matter of faith. We believe it because we believe it. That argument wouldn't go far in a scientist's lab or a court of law, but even a scientist or attorney will acknowledge the existence of his own thoughts and feelings. Can the same belief or "faith" be applied to a possibility like God? I don't see why not. Thus, I am an agnostic theist.

March 4, 2013... Lord of the Kings

With the passing of David, his son Sol'o-mon is given great wisdom by God and rules over Israel for many years... largely in peace. He becomes renowned for his wise judgments and compassionate disposition... and is respected and loved by all...for a while. The account of his rise and reign is detailed and interesting, and, for the most part, without serious criticism. I do, however, wonder about the wisdom of someone who would have 700 wives. Joke aside, in 1 Kings 8:65 there is mention of a great feast to celebrate the completion of the first permanent "house" of the Lord... that lasts either seven days or fourteen days (I'm not sure). On the eighth day, Sol'o-mon sends the celebrants home. As before, I wonder about the supposedly mandatory observance of the Sabbath... which is not mentioned.

Since Sol'o-mon is blessed with the wisdom of the Lord, I find it somewhat perplexing that he becomes corrupted by wealth... and his illegal non-Hebrew wives, and takes up the acknowledgment of other Gods and their respective idols. I wonder where his great wisdom was when that happened. Can it be possible that God's gift of wisdom was not what He made it out to be? Could God have purposely graced Sol'o-mon with faulty wisdom? ...knowing full well that he would go afoul in the long run? If so, why then would He chastise and punish Sol'o-mon for doing precisely what He planned? If God did not mean for Sol'o-mon to be corrupted, why then was he? After around 500 years of the chosen ones going astray time after time, one is forced to wonder about the wisdom of God, Himself, in choosing the chosen ones. I also marvel that God felt compelled to choose a people at all... for any reason. What is the point of it? They repeatedly disappoint Him. He repeatedly gets angry and punishes them. The very numerous other peoples of the earth don't seem to be placed on the earth (by God?) for any particular reason... other than the continued frustration of the Lord's own work. How can it be that God created a troublesome people who are troubled by other troublesome people... all of whom are troublesome to God, and who constantly get in trouble for doing it? "Believers" often say things like, "We mere humans cannot possibly understand the workings of the Lord." I say, however, that it appears to me that God, Himself, doesn't fully understand what is going on. Who among us would purposely create problems for ourselves, get angry when the problems occurred, and then throw a tantrum in response to it? Seriously, is this the kind of God I should be impressed with?

March 6, 2013... Kings and Prophets

First Kings, despite my previous comments, is actually a relatively respectful account of the various Kings and prophets that followed after Sol'o-mon. There is a considerable amount of detail and legitimacy in its telling. Second Kings, on the other hand... although I am only a short way into it, is beginning to look somewhat curious to me. I am loathe to comment prematurely, having progressed only a few pages into it, but am compelled to make mention of a couple of interesting occurrences.

E-li'jah was known and accepted as a prophet of God in 1-Kings... and as such, was in conversation with Him on many occasions. His fame as a prophet was derived from this established relationship he apparently had with the Lord. Prophets, in fact, generally were validated by the demonstrated manifestation of their prophecies. I was, therefore, just a little surprised to find that, like Joshua, E-li'jah parted the Jordan River shortly before a chariot (and horses) of fire appeared to whisk him off to heaven. One might say he went out in a blaze of glory.

Oh, and one more thing regarding E-li'jah... unless I missed something, he appears to be the only human being (so far) that found his way into heaven without having died first. It is perhaps too early in my reading to make a comment on this, but unless I am mistaken, even Jesus wasn't able to claim that particular feat... though I realize He was meant to die on our behalf. Interesting.

With the death of E-li'jah, E-li'sha became the blessed recipient of the Lord's spirit... and consequently inherited e-li'jah's status as primary prophet. The interesting and curious things that happened thereafter are intriguing... primarily due to the fact that I have never in my life heard of these "miracles"... whether due to my ignorance or some dogmatic minimization. E-li'sha, too, parted the Jordan River... obviously a much more achievable task than the famous trick of Moses. But then I was surprised that he also raised the dead son of a woman who was kind to him... and cured Na'a-man of leprosy. It seems to me that another famous prophet performed very similar miracles later in the Bible... to a much more celebrated effect. My curiosity is piqued by this seemingly divine (or divinely empowered) man. I will look forward, with considerable interest, to the remainder of 2-Kings.

March 7, 2013... A Matter of Life and Death

It occurred to me today, as I slogged through 2-Kings, that murder, sanctioned or otherwise, appears to be the overriding theme throughout not only this book, but many of the previous ones, as well. There is killing on nearly every page. It is almost as though everyone is either a killer or a killee. Wholesale slaughter is probably the most conspicuous occurrence I have encountered in the entire Old Testament so far. Entire cities are totally destroyed... men, women, children, donkeys, and goats. Fathers kill sons. Sons kill fathers. Treachery and murder are not only practiced by the dastardly villains but sanctioned by God and performed with zeal by the chosen ones. The chosen ones are not particularly discriminating in their choice of victims, either. They kill each other with abandon. Unless I am mistaken, I would swear that Thou Shalt Not Kill is one of the fundamental commandments of God... yet God, Himself, not only encourages killings at every turn, He uses just about any excuse to kill someone... usually by "the edge of the sword"... and often by the dozens or thousands. What kind of religion is this? Where is the sanctity of life I have heard about? If life is of such little value, how is a person supposed to accept that God is a merciful God? If Kings was the last book of the Bible, I can say with absolute honesty that I would promptly dispose of it as an absurd example of the incredible ignorance and cruelty of the human race... and the contradictory and immoral ridiculousness of their God(s).

I am certainly not qualified to pass judgment... for the perusal of others... on the validity of the Christian religion... and readers are quite free to form their own opinions regarding the Old Testament, but for my part, I find it offensive and perverse and ridiculously pointless. If ever there was a story based on a true story, this is it in my eyes... with the emphasis on "based".

I really do not know where the morality comes from that I live by. I am sure that a measure of it stems from early Sunday school sessions in my youth, and although there are certainly moral lessons in the Bible (if one were to use a discriminating filter to find them), up to Kings, I have found little of redeeming value. If I were to make a chart with examples of a desirable morality in one column, and examples of undesirable morality in another, I have no doubt that the undesirable side of the chart would spill onto many pages, while the "good" side would be sadly lacking in content. One might discern from my comments that I am not happy with the Bible so far... and one would be correct.

Again, though, with respect for the billions of Christian believers... some of which are more learned than me, it would be grossly wrong of me to form my final opinions regarding the Bible after having read only a third of it. I will reassure any potential readers that I am not a lost cause. I am not giving up my quest. I am not putting up a brick wall to what I will find on subsequent pages. I still, very much, want to find spiritual value and validity as I progress through the great book. I have not given up hope.

March 13, 2013... An Enigma of Understanding

From my small beginnings in rural southwestern Wisconsin to my equally small, but current, place among my fellow human beings in southwestern Wisconsin, I have somehow developed an understanding of the world and its workings that is likely as questionable as the questions it has spawned. That is to say that I feel nearly as distant from any real enlightenment as I felt a decade ago when I discovered that I possessed a great and all-to-obvious ignorance about just about everything. The more I learn, the more I yearn for more.

Ten years ago, almost to the day, I experienced a personal revelation that resulted in the beginnings of what I consider to be a new life. One might say that I (slowly) became born again... although not in a religious sense, but rather regarding the acknowledgment of, and wrestlings with, my own ignorance... and the dysfunctional mess it had made of my life. The untangling of my life's work notwithstanding, I also realized that there was a conspicuous void inside that should have been the residence of my spiritual identity. Somehow, during the course of my quirky early life, I had hidden my own intangible soul behind barriers that I, myself, had built up and maintained... and which gave me a distinct and pervading sense that something was missing all the time. This very journal is part of my on-going effort to reestablish my intangible existence to its rightful place and make it grow... as it should have been doing all along. Better late than never.

As I mentioned earlier, being of a "western" persuasion, many of the names and places I encounter in the Bible are not only difficult to pronounce but also nearly impossible to retain in my memory. My friends will attest to the sad history and efficacy of my memory. A basic necessity, then... to aid in my understanding and absorption of Biblical details, is occasional reinforcement. Just as Deuteron-omy was a review of sorts, of the Pentateuch, Chronicles 1 & 2 serve as a review of the historical events that occurred from David through the four hundred years or so after him. It helps... and I can't help but believe that it has helped many people through the centuries. A reasonable understanding and retention of the chronological events simply makes for a more complete story... if nothing else. Whether or not a reader of the Bible actually buys into everything presented there is another issue. Hopefully, it will be understood that my God-given ignorance, skepticism, and subsequent yearnings for spiritual completeness are, in my eyes, every bit as valid as the overwhelmingly accepted story unfolding in the Bible.

March 16, 2013... Good and Evil

It occurred to me as I work my way through the Biblical review and elaborations found in Chronicles, that most of the kings that are mentioned did evil in the sight of the Lord... with a few exceptions. This seems to be primarily in regard to the recognition and worship of other Gods. When God favored Moses with the ten commandments (twice), He did not, if I remember accurately, prioritize any of them, but I have noticed as I advance further into the Bible that He seems to be considerably more concerned with the worship of other Gods than with any of the other commandments... though there are occasional trespasses that get noticed... such as David's "coveting" of someone else's wife. As I mentioned in a previous journal entry, there is a conspicuous amount of killing going on that doesn't seem to bother God much in the least. In fact, He seems to get in on the action much more than I, personally, deem necessary. One person sins, and God kills seventy thousand people. I realize that the Old Testament is based on the fear of God, but I am seeing words like "merciful" being used to describe Him... He most certainly is not... by any stretch of the imagination.

This also brings me, once again, to the contentious point I mentioned earlier. Why would God create an imperfect people, then condemn them when they manifest their imperfections, and penalize thousands of innocent others who had nothing, whatsoever, to do with any of it. Some points bear repeating... for effect. This is one of them. This does not look like mysterious ways to me... it looks like God makes mistakes. Were we not made in His image?

I also have to question the "good" I have encountered. David comes to mind here, as well. David is revered as one of the most favored kings of the chosen ones. He demonstrates, more than once, that he is not willing to kill Saul, God's anointed first king... despite the fact that Saul tries on more than one occasion to kill David. How can Saul be seen as "good" enough to deserve protection when he is dead bent on murdering David? How can David be seen as "good" when he refuses to rid his people of this anointed lunatic that has chronic killing on his brain. David jump-started his status by defeating Goliath, and became a king that was generally kind and respectful and well-loved, but his reign was riddled with war, infighting, infidelity, murder, and chaos. Yet, he was (or is) cherished as one of the greatest kings of Israel. To be perfectly honest, I was quite surprised and dismayed that David was not the role model I had expected. He had good qualities, to be sure, but I certainly would not classify him as the standout and reverential king he is made out to be. Other kings were put to death for lesser sins than David's.

It also occurs to me that good and evil, in general, are subjective and elusive terms to nail down. Who, exactly, is the final authority... qualified to make the call? If people elect a judge to pass judgments, are the judgments just... simply because of an election? If we, the people, are not qualified to make these judgments on our own... and elect or appoint a judge to do it for us, wouldn't our choices for judge be as questionable as the judgments we might otherwise make? If I am capable of making mistakes, and I appoint someone else to make judgments for me...

who is also capable of making mistakes, is it not entirely possible that the judg-ments, themselves, are occasionally likely to be mistakes? If God chose Saul to be the first king of Israel... complete with promises to exalt him forever... and then Saul turns out to have been a bad choice, does it not appear that God made a mistake?

So now it appears that we (or at least the chosen ones) were, indeed, created in God's image. We are imperfect and make mistakes... likewise, so is God. Blas-phemy? Perhaps... but I admit my ignorance... and am repenting offenses in the interest of learning. My search for spiritual validity demands that I question what is before me and discuss (with myself, at least) what my possibilities are. I should think that an earnest search for my intangible existence is an honorable enough undertaking that wrong turns, bumps in the road, and bad directions are both understandable and excusable.

March 20, 2013... A Scribe Described

Though I have no serious issues with the book of Ezra, it has come to my attention that a question exists regarding the order of books... which came first, Ezra or Nehemiah? The King James Bible places Ezra first... and that is good enough for the likes of me. As I understand it, not having read Nehemiah as yet, one is essen-tially an embellishment of the other. I will probably have more to say regarding this after I have actually read Nehemiah. For now, though, it is irrelevant to me.

Although I am not perfectly clear on the reasons that the king of Babylon sud-denly decided to free his captives and slaves of seventy years, he apparently did... with not only his blessings but also his financing. Ezra leads the remnants of the chosen ones... now called the Jews, back to Jerusalem to rebuild the house of God. There are complications and the work is delayed, but it is eventually finished and celebrated with the newly resurrected rituals of sacrifice and Passover. Ezra is frus-trated, however, with the intermarriages that occurred during the exile and slavery of his people. He prostrates himself and pleads with God for mercy... in light of the "sins" committed. Although I did not discern a response from the Almighty, I do find it a bit strange that God, who is often described as merciful, seems to hold

fast to his laws and statutes... with no regard for the fact that his people were captured, displaced from their "promised land", and enslaved for seventy years with
little hope for rescue or redemption. I should think it would be somewhat understandable that they would intermingle with the people of Babylon over time. Ezra,
however, makes a covenant with God to purge the pagans from their midst... dis-
solving the sinful marriages and alienating their own children. Apparently, the
children of these "mixed" marriages, although half chosen, were not chosen
enough to be accepted by God... innocent or not. God insisted on a pure lineage
of Jews. I sort of remember Hitler thinking along these same lines regarding his
Aryan race.

March 21, 2013... Nehemiah's Story

I mentioned, in the previous passage, that I did not know why the king of Babylon
suddenly decided to allow the Jews to return to Jerusalem. I have since come to
realize that the Persians conquered Babylon and the "new" king, Cyrus... and later
Darius chose to accommodate the Jews in their wish to rebuild the temple in Jerusalem. There were apparently two groups of chosen ones who returned to Jerusalem... one with Ezra, with the blessings of Cyrus, and the other with Nehemiah
with the blessings of Darius. The temple was rebuilt and, later, the city walls and
homes within Jerusalem.

As I stated earlier, I have no significant issues with the story of Ezra and Nehemiah, but it does seem to be a curious coincidence that I have encountered this
particular part of the Bible at this time. I think I mentioned that I am also reading
Gore Vidal's Creation, which is a historical novel based at this very same location
and time... although the adventures of the Jews is not part of Vidal's story. The
characters of Cyrus and Darius... and the cities of Babylon and Susa and others are
mentioned... giving a helpful perspective on the history of the area and the time of
these events.

March 22, 2013... To Be or Not To Be... Dead

A few months ago, I happened onto a talk radio program in which a brain cancer surgeon/author was being interviewed about his new book concerning his repeated encounters with patients who died... and then "came back". Sam Parnia's book, What Happens When We Die was more than a simple curiosity to me. It promised to address such things as soul, spirit, consciousness, life and death. I promptly ordered the book, read it with great anticipation, and pondered... at least for a while... the implications of life before and after death. Dr. Parnia presented many accounts by his own patients of their "near-death" experiences... which he became convinced were not only real, but quite profound and singular life-changing events. There were simply too many to discount... with too many similarities common to them all to be dismissed as coincidences. In each case, the dead, or dying, patients were able to recall things that happened to them and around them... even though they were clinically dead. They felt their spirits moving and became aware of other spirits who had died previously... even before their own births. They were able to describe things they could not possibly have known. Some even saw God. Upon their "return", they were no longer fearful of their own death. They were wholeheartedly convinced that death was simply a largely pleasant transition to a different level of existence. They all seemed to experience something that magnified and clarified the overwhelming importance and value of love. This was interesting stuff.

As is usually the case with me and my endeavors, I moved on to something else and let the brief "tickle" of curiosity fade... until now. Since then, through the influence of others who are close to me, I have again begun to investigate the possibilities for spiritual discovery... and the validity of faith-based beliefs. Out of some dusty back room of my brain, I have stumbled upon Dr. Parnia's book again... only to find myself researching some of the other claims regarding near-death experiences. It is very disheartening to realize that whatever bewitching and intriguing information I might find will still wallow in uncertainty and skepticism... lacking proof, and testing credibility. It is becoming fairly clear to me that a new and different set of tools are needed to evaluate the universe of the intangible. Where might I find these tools? Do they exist at all? Is it simply impossible for mere humans to evolve to a level where intangible existence is perceivable and measurable and understandable? I have heard that we human beings only use a very small portion of the potential of our brains. It occurs to me that, likewise, we also use a comparatively small portion of our minds. This is truly unfortunate if it is true, but I hope, not beyond our redeeming capabilities. This entire intangible adventure of mine into the smoky world of uncertainty and unfortunate debate is my attempt to bridge what is known and what is not. I do not wish to simply feel without knowing why. I can't accept that I am able to think for no apparent reason. Not knowing does not mean not knowable. Ignorant does not mean dumb.

March 23, 2013... Esther

To date, I have found few "stories" in the Great Book that are told compellingly without miracles and fanciful legendy embellishments. The story of Esther is obviously a continuation of the books of Ezra and Nehemiah and is refreshingly believable... even without researching the validity of the story... which I am sure, many scholars have already done. I have no reason to question what is written in Esther. In a way, it is a classic "good guys win" story... assuming the Jews who remained in Babylon were the good guys.

March 25, 2013... The Perplexity and Challenge of Job

In the interest of honesty, I find that I must once again proclaim ignorance regarding my understanding of the Book of Job. In fact, I am not sure, having read it, that it is possible for one such as me to fathom its meaning or reason for being. It was a surprise, to be sure, to encounter such a Shakespearean confusion... after half a Bible's worth of relatively straightforward... if not believable... stories. It will likely be clear, to anyone who reads my comments, that I simply do not know where to start my discussion of Job... or in what direction it should progress.

Although I am somewhat drawn to the poetic style Job exhibits, I found it sort of out of place in an otherwise reasonably clearly written history. Obviously, the flowery dialog between Job and his "friends" was deemed relevant in the eyes of Biblical scholars long ago. My initial confusion upon reading it caused me to do a bit of research in an effort to at least understand a little of what its purpose is in the Great Book. I am not certain, however, if I achieved that understanding.

My first question pertains to the estimated time of origin for this book. It doesn't seem to be clear who wrote it... it has even been attributed to Moses... although I doubt it, or when it was written... although I saw one source claiming it was from around 2,100 B.C. If this is true, why did it seem sensible to insert it into the Bible after a mostly chronological history that starts with creation and leads to approximately 400 B.C.? I realize that Job is a section unto itself... unrelated to the Biblical history presented to this point, except for its related ubiquitous theme of God testing man. I think my feelings regarding this point have been expressed well enough. I guess I have known since before I began reading the Bible that the books were not necessarily in a strict chronological order. I, therefore, am not overly concerned with the issue of when it was written... or by whom for that matter. I have mentioned it as a mere point of curiosity.

Shakespearean dialog aside, I found the drawn out speeches of each of the participants in the discussions tedious and almost excruciatingly overstated. Like Job, himself, I agonized over why he was "tested" in the first place. God knew he was a good man (didn't He?). Satan, who makes an unexpected sudden appearance in the story, tempts God into allowing the torture of someone who has done nothing wrong. Where did Satan come from all of sudden? Why did God allow Himself to be tempted by him? Is God not observant enough of Satan's methods that He allows Himself to be swayed by an obviously evil entity? If God could command Satan to restrict his torment of Job, could He not also command Satan to...well...go to Hell?

One of my sources of explanation referred to Satan (in this story) as meaning "adversary". Up until this point in the chronology, God has made it abundantly clear that He does not tolerate adversaries. Why, then, is Satan tolerated? Why are Satan's works worthy of God's consideration at all? How can the Lord be manipulated into doing tests on His faithful followers by a known deviant? Why do I wonder why, when I was obviously created to wonder why, but expected to accept on faith the absurdities I find everywhere? It appears that one purpose of the book of Job is to teach us mere humans that the workings of the Lord are mysterious and that we cannot possibly understand the why of it all. Why, then, were we given the ability and wherewithal to wonder why? …so that we will learn faith? If I am to understand that God can't be understood, then how can I be expected to understand how faith works… or even if it does work? Why would God rely on a concept as elusive and un-understandable as faith? How might I possibly be regarded as ungodly when I was never meant to know what that means? Why do I yearn for understanding when it is supposedly beyond my capability to understand?

I realize that faith is a capability that all human beings seem to be capable of… at least I have faith that we do. If this is true, then it seems reasonable that our faith might be expected to be directed in some direction or another. It also seems reasonable that whatever we happen to have faith in is likely something that cannot be directly substantiated or validated by proofs… otherwise, faith would not be needed. So if faith is possible, expected, and appropriate in certain cases, who, exactly, is qualified to determine if it is used in a valid way or misdirected… as is so obviously a human trait? Our human history is peppered with more than enough examples of misplaced faith to justify my questions regarding it. Am I to declare my faith in whatever I choose without fear of recrimination by others? Am I to suffer the inevitable confusion that input from others will most assuredly produce? …since we have a considerable history of not agreeing with each other on nearly everything we think of, believe in, or practice. How can anyone decide on a faith-based path to follow… knowing full well that there are absolutely no measurable criteria on which to make a decision? It seems to me that only a closed-minded and ignorant thinker would make a choice such as this based on the suggestions, pleadings, or commands of others… whether large numbers of believers happen to accept it or not. We simply have been wrong too many times in the past to trust our individual or collective judgments. Do we really wish to be forever plagued by our own inability to learn from past mistakes? I truly hope not. I am an agnostic because of possibilities. How can that be faulted? …even by God… who created possibilities and supposedly made me this way.

Although three of Job's friends visit him in the story to encourage him to repent his sins and criticize God, a fourth also appears. After long-drawn-out tirades by

Job and his three friends, Elihu, the fourth, chastises all for berating God. Finally, God joins the conversation and demonstrates to Job that he cannot possibly understand the workings of the Lord. God also speaks directly to the three friends... commanding them to sacrifice in repentance for their misdirected advice. Lastly, God restores Job's possessions (double) and gives him a new family to replace what was taken from him... and blesses him with favor and long life.

The problems I find here, aside from what I already mentioned, have to do with several details of the story. After all was said and done, Elihu, who as near as I could discern, was good and right in the eyes of the Lord, simply disappeared at the end... as mysteriously as he appeared. He was not recognized by God as righteous or rewarded or even sent on his way with blessings. He just vanished. The three friends, although quite critical of both Job and God... in no uncertain terms, got off easy with a burnt offering. Job, the innocent victim in the story, suffered greatly, while his "friends" were penalized for their sins with a big feast.

My most bothersome problem in the story regards Satan. After God's query, he is described as having come from "going to and fro in the earth, and from walking up and down in it." (Job:7) First, why did God have to ask Satan where he came from? Did He not know? During God's long-winded and (I thought) quite arrogant and self-aggrandizing speech to Job later, He made it quite clear that He knows all... yet He did not seem to know the comings and goings of Satan. Satan, too, simply disappears from concern at the end of the story. He tempted God directly and purposely... lied about Job...causing much grief and torment... and got away with it without so much as a final mention. It seems to me that the moral of the story leaves out the biggest perpetrator... the instigator of the whole thing. Nice flowery language, though.

April 2, 2013... A Perplexing Overabundance of Praise

Any reader who may have suffered through this journal to this point will have certainly noticed that I struggle with many issues regarding the Old Testament. Now as I labor through Psalms, I find myself wondering why the assemblers of the Bible chose to insert one hundred and fifty prayers into it... that seem, to my eyes, quite tedious and unnecessarily repetitious... not to mention biased. To be honest, after forty or so psalms, I found it really quite difficult to slog through the remaining 110. Praise is all well and good. I understand and respect the desire for it... and the questionable benefits of it (brown-nosing God notwithstanding), but I cannot, for the life of me, explain, justify or enjoy this unnecessary barrage of repetitive commentary. It, in no way, demonstrates anything of significance to me. It is largely, in my eyes, an exhaustive string of one-sided opinions and pleadings that real human beings passionately expounded (supposedly)... and which were apparently recorded, word for word (by unsubstantiated someones), for the benefit of posterity. Horse feathers.

April 27, 2013... A Consideration of Time

I have found, perplexingly, that occasional thoughts of interest seem to fall out of nowhere at the most unseemly of times. I have, for instance, written a few of my better-crafted songs...while driving. Inspiration (whatever that is) often manifests itself while I am waiting for my wife to "get ready" for something. There doesn't appear to be any discernible pattern for the appearance of these rather pleasing mental candies. If there was some way to make them happen, I would do so regularly and with uncharacteristic zeal. As it is, though, I am resigned to accept the occasional pleasantness as the mysterious surprise that it is. One such thoughtful surprise visited me this morning while the family dog was being coaxed into her pen.

Einstein posited that time is one of four dimensions created when the universe was born (...or begat?). Unlike Einstein, though, who not only tended to develop and ponder questions, but also attempted to answer them, I simply dig out questions that undoubtedly have already been asked by others, ponder them, and then leave them for some as yet undetermined scorekeeper to tally in hopes that the questions, themselves, eventually might lead my thinking in a valid direction. Validity, then, is my goal... not answers (necessarily) to unanswerable questions.

If there was no time before the beginning of time, what WAS there? Scientists have determined that the universe is 13.8 billion years old. If time started then (and Einstein was correct), then a finite point of beginning happened. If God snapped His fingers (once a day for six days, supposedly), and created the universe... time and all, then there absolutely WAS a beginning point. If that is true (...and who knows?), then I should think that God would have gotten the idea to create the universe BEFORE He actually did it. That being the case, there had to be time before time... or there couldn't be a before at all. Perhaps there was a different kind of time. Godtime, perhaps. Foolish musings.

The thought that struck me this morning, though, had to do with Einstein's idea that time is a dimension. It might be remembered that I also suggested for consideration that our intangible existence might also be, or reside in, another dimension. It actually seems equally as plausible to me that our consciousness, or spirit, is part of another dimension as yet undetectable... as that time is. In fact, it is considerably more palatable to me than the abstract idea of a divine residence for our spirits... unless, of course, God is ALSO another dimension... or in one.

Another point of contention concerns the possibility of a real past and future. Like many of the ideas I have been thinking about, there don't seem to be clear and concise definitions for these phenomena. That being the case, I will take the liberty of defining them myself. I will say, then, that the past is simply a present that has happened and which can be documented. I will likewise say that the future is simply a present that has not happened and which cannot be documented. As I stated earlier: interpretation is everything... and I reserve the right to interpret as fully and freely as anyone else.

Generally, scientists (physicists), agree that the past and future are illusions of the mind. The only reality is the present one... which although fleeting, is the only one that few can deny. According to my definitions, though, I would have to take issue with this. Since my view states that the past can be documented, it can be shown by our own record that a reality has passed and is verifiable. Our individual perception of the past is where the contention comes into play. As I said, interpretation is a free right.

What strikes me as strange, though, is that Einstein explains time as a real dimension of the universe... accepted by physicists everywhere. But those same phys-

icists proclaim that the past and future are illusions. If the present is the only reality, and the past and future are not real and do not exist, then time would have to
be defined as a perpetual present... negating the historical record of documented
past realities. In other words, time doesn't exist. Einstein wasn't right about everything, but he was right about enough that I, personally, would not want to go up
against him. Woe to the physicists who do.

So where am I going with all of this? I am not absolutely sure... since I tend to
think as I write. Somewhere down the line, I hope to develop a way of thinking
about these intangible ideas that doesn't rely on speculation or faith so much as an
educated hypothesis. What I call critical thinking is essential in this cause. In the
absence of tangible proofs, I have no recourse but to base my desired spiritual path
on the best combination of earnestly wrung-out ideas and questions. I am not
trying to draw a relationship between time and spirituality. I am investigating the
understandability of intangible similarities... and including whatever might fall
into the intangible category on the way. Time and faith seem like two completely
unrelated things, but there do seem to be similarities with regard to what is known
and what is assumed and what is simply opinion. Should I believe in God? ...or
the future? I defy anyone to verify either.

April 28, 2013... The Wisdom of Proverbs

It is interesting that the book of Proverbs encourages the fostering of wisdom...
and even defines, in a biased way, what wisdom is... colored (as it were) with the
principal theme of the fear of God. My borderline issue with this is simply that I
don't happen to believe that wisdom is only attained or practiced by God-fearing
individuals. To imply that is to have an arrogant and narrow-minded Christian
bias (which the Bible obviously has). Some might say that any faith-based belief
requires a certain dedication to its principles which could be construed as arrogance and bias. Although it could be true, I prefer, for no particularly good reason,
to simply say that to believe a certain way is a personal choice. There are those who
will, no doubt, be brainwashed or heavily influenced... others who will be noncommittal or unsure, but ultimately it still comes down to personal choice, however, or whyever, the choice was made.

One definition of proverbs that I looked up described them as truths that are not always or entirely true. I immediately saw this as a singularly appropriate oxymoron. If ever there was an explanation suited for the Bible, this was it. Another definition described them as "generally accepted wisdom in the form of memorable sayings". I tend to favor this definition since it avoids the testy meaning of truths.

April 30, 2013... The Proverbial Book of Vanity

Ecclesiastes struck me as somewhat strange and a bit out-of-place in The Bible. The fact that the author is not clear appears to me as one point of mild contention since the lessons put forth, although meaningful, seem to come from someone who is obsessed with vanity. Everything is vanity. Do something and you are vain. Don't do something and you are vain. Get begat and you will eventually die and everything in between is all vanity. "To everything, there is a season..."... not exactly profound wisdom... though it makes for a wonderful song hook.

There is conjecture that Solomon authored the book, though it is attributed to "the preacher". Regardless of the origins of the writings, the point seems to be that after all is said and done, only the acceptance of, and praise for, God can make life meaningful and successful... despite our best intentions without Him. We may convince ourselves that we are knowledgeable or wise or generous... or we might see ourselves as possessing other positive attributes, but ultimately only our faith in God will allow us to be judged righteous and worthy of Him. I realize that these proverbs are an extension of what is taught throughout the Bible, but they DO remind me of one particularly bothersome characteristic that people seem to flaunt without regard for critical thinking. I am talking about the tendency of people to proclaim a belief as though it is an accepted and established fact. While essentially all of the proverbs are generally valid... even the ones that contradict, they seem to assume that every human thought and action can be controlled or affected by our own human choices... which is certainly not the case. Accidents happen. Things happen TO us randomly. We make unintended mistakes... and so do others. We simply cannot avoid doing what might be construed as vain things all the time. And who is to decide what is vain? God has been incommunicado for centuries.

His proponents are all too vocal, but who, exactly, possesses the authority... sanctioned by God... to judge his fellow human beings? What is vanity in the eyes of God? Are there excusable, mitigating circumstances that take into account the variability of human behaviors, intentions, accidents, and redemption? It has been my experience... such as it is, that the human-ordained religious leaders (vanity?) mull over questions such as these and make rules to live by based on their interpretations of Christian dogma, rather than any kind of actual divine instruction. As a fellow human being with the exact same potential capabilities for divine interpretation, I reserve the right to determine for myself what is vain and what is not. But...that too is vanity.

May 2, 2013... The Song and Dance of Solomon

I have to admit to a certain ignorance in my choice to discuss the various books of the Bible with only myself... and possibly some unseen potential future reader. Had I the benefit of scholarly theological lessons, I would likely have appreciated the book of Song of Solomon to a greater degree. However, since the Bible is meant for common people (who are all-too-often ignorant), I thought it appropriate to read it as I am. The learned assemblers of the Great Book, no doubt, pondered which of the many writings at their disposal should be included... and their well-reasoned decisions regarding inclusions were certainly debated, thoroughly studied, and thoughtfully interpreted... I am sure. I am also sure that those who proclaim themselves in charge sometimes formulate opinions and make decisions based on nothing but vanity, untested whims and arrogance, and agendas. Anyone who has had a boss will know what I mean.

As a poet and songwriter, I feel that I am qualified, at least in some small way, to comment on the Song of Solomon with a measure of confidence that might otherwise be lacking. My pragmatic agnostic side, however, demands that I take a more negatively critical stance than most people probably would. It is, after all, a love song/poem between two lovers... purportedly Solomon, himself, and his new bride, the nameless Shulammite girl. Love is dripping from nearly every line. The marriage is celebrated with undiluted and exuberant exultations of love... and although parallels to the love of God can be drawn easily enough, it is plainly an unabashed proclamation of love by two young lovers. They are in love. They get married. They are happy.

I seem to remember, though... if I can be so bold, that Solomon had 700 wives... and a large number of concubines, as well. It seems to me that his undying love must have had to be spread somewhat thinly across the harem. His great wisdom appears to be shadowed only by his great number of wives and lovers. Perhaps, if my irreverence is not too unpalatable, the book should have been called the Schlong of Solomon.

May 9, 2013... Agnostic Prejudice and Incredulous Piety

It has been my (not altogether surprising) experience that whosoever believeth in the Bible is biased toward its validity as the de facto established and confirmed word of God. Generally, it also appears that those who believe this are not open to other possibilities... however possible they might be. They (the believers) also seem (to me) to be somewhat arrogant in the righteousness of their thinking... although I fully realize that we all tend to be defensive about the way we think. I will reiterate that I am trying very hard to be a good skeptic... that is, one that will keep an open mind regarding possibilities, and who will, as gracefully as possible, accept compelling ideas... even when they go against what I may have previously thought. This journal of my thoughts IS a search for ideas that I may not have considered in the past. It IS my attempt to allow the arguments of others, however different they might be from my own, to be considered as valid criteria in developing a spiritual direction for myself. However skeptical, or agnostic, or arrogant, or wrong I might seem to others, I truly am attempting to honestly address the blank, unfulfilled parts of my intangible existence in an effort to fill them with the most valid beliefs (if not proofs) that I reasonably can with whatever resources I am able to muster toward that goal. It is actually a tall order...one that I essentially do not see others attempting, for the most part... although I am sure there are those who do attempt it in their own behind-the-scenes world. So far though, most of the people I have discussed my "project" with, do not seem to understand why I don't simply allow myself to believe as they do. They tell me it would be a lot easier to just accept things without too much concern for the "details". They say that I will never see the benefits of faith if I don't allow myself to have it... while trying to hash out details that cannot be understood or reconciled by mere humans. I understand what they are saying, but if I am not mistaken, their description of faith closely resembles the definition of brainwashing. Opinions aside, for me personally, I cannot discount possibilities simply because they get in the way and can be troublesome. I am not willing to commit my "eternal soul" to an idea that doesn't seem to be based on anything that I can understand. I do not think it unreasonable to doubt when I was, after all, made to, and made to have the capability to doubt. Skepticism is the only real tool I have as a fail-safe against brainwashing... which has been all too prevalent in the historical past. How can I be faulted for whatever ignorance I display when I very apparently was MADE to be ignorant. I also, however, was created with the wherewithal to overcome my ignorance (and emptiness of spirit) through skepticism, learning, and (sigh) faith.

Why, then, did I choose to expound another disclaimer? Simply this... The Book of Isaiah, in my opinion, is a confusing, convoluted, unnecessarily tedious example of why interpretation is an absolute requirement for any self-respecting Christian who might claim to glean any meaning, whatsoever, from it. I am sure there are some who would laugh at my naiveté and foolhardy conclusions, but I consider myself a reasonably average person with fairly normal capacities for discerning meaning from what I read. If the Bible was meant for "regular" people to use as a guide for living, and to find salvation... and I think that it was, it is my wholehearted opinion that it fails miserably. Chosen or not, people were created (somehow) to be imperfect. How can we possibly be expected, by any reasonably intelligent God, to exercise anything resembling proper judgments with regard to our beliefs or faiths when we were meant to make mistakes, be doubtful, throw caution to the wind, succumb to temptations, just plain get mad, and even justify pretty much everything we do, think or say... good or bad? I defy anyone to find an answer to that question in the Book of Isaiah.

It also occurs to me that there are only a handful of "prophets" who supposedly conversed with God. Those human beings (remember...the imperfect ones) are the ones who wrote down their sacred conversations... in most cases, word-for-word... with real quotes no less, for posterity to benefit from. If the Lord is so vehemently insistent that people (at least the chosen ones) conform to His ways without fail (or else), why would He place their salvation into the hands of a very few imperfect human scribes/priests... when He could just as well have simply spoken His expectations to the masses en masse? Why the go-betweens? Why the interpretation? Why was it a part of God's plan to give people the gift of choice... and then punish them if they made the wrong one? Why were mistakes not forgiven when we were created to make them?

My brief research into the Book of Isaiah tells me that there is considerable speculation as to who actually wrote it. Most agree that Isaiah did indeed write the first part... which details events that happened during his lifetime. Some say that he also wrote the second part which deals with the Babylonian wars in which Jerusalem fell and the Hebrews became slaves in Babylon or were scattered... and then set free to return... even though this occurred after Isaiah died. Some also say he wrote the parts that are (plainly?) interpreted to foretell the coming of Christ. Many clues, however, point to the probability that at least three different people wrote the book... evidenced by different styles and references contained in the sections. Regardless of who wrote the book, it is still very much evident to me that the historical references are mostly valid... however accurate they may be, but the intense warnings from God (Yahweh), the mostly vague and somewhat questionable "hints" of what was to come, and the insistence of total acceptance or death... is of some suspicion to me. God seems (as documented by the prophet) to exhibit a propensity for making dire threats. It has been demonstrated over and over throughout the Old Testament up to this Book (so far). Why were the chosen ones chosen? Why are we expected to believe that the Hebrews were chosen? ...because the Hebrews said they were? Had I been alive back then... and conveniently in the vicinity, I would promptly have stood up and proclaimed, "Really? God told me the EXACT same thing!" ...and then I would soon produce the written record of the whole conversation to "prove" it.

I have wondered, on occasion, about how the sudden reemergence of a legitimate prophet might be accepted in this modern world we live in. Is it possible that one of the many schizophrenics currently residing in a padded hotel somewhere is a bona fide prophet whose voices are the sacred conversation of a very real God?

Might one of the countless unfortunate mentally ill people who are doped to acceptable tolerance be, in actuality, desperately attempting to transmit God's updated and badly needed modern message? Has the second coming, perhaps, come and gone... deflected by the well-meaning sequestering of an obviously insane messiah? I suspect that it would take a miracle to convince an overly skeptical public that a modern-day person might, indeed, be an agent of the Lord. Personally, I would accept something less than a miracle as a convincing argument if I had more to go on than a hodgepodge of fantastical stories and self-endorsed "messages".

The "main event", though, is obviously the prophecy of the coming of Christ (7:14). Although this particular part of Isaiah is compelling enough, there are things that haunt my understanding of it... and which I will discuss with myself as best I can. The Book of Isaiah is fairly long... and despite the concerns I have mentioned already, there are an agonizing few more.

In the book, it is repeated over and over...and over...how great and powerful God is... page after page of it. There is also an inordinate amount of praise, more than enough warnings, and a fair amount of confusing and vague talk of a "new" earth and a "new" heaven. A two thousand year hindsight, and a couple of millennia of interpretations, has led us to believe that at some point in our future (or maybe only the chosen one's future) things will be so different and pleasant that we will lose our memory of our long and not-so-glorious past. Isaiah (or whoever wrote it) was an optimist. Amidst all of this bragging, praise & warnings there is suddenly inserted one sentence that we are expected to believe predicts the cataclysmic altering of the fate of all human beings forever. Isaiah 7:14 (supposedly written hundreds of years before Christ) foretells His coming...kind of. In Isaiah, He is to be born to a virgin and called Immanuel. Since I have encountered more than one instance of people in the Bible with more than one name, it is not terribly difficult for me to accept that Jesus could be called by two names... especially in light of the apparent tendency in those days for names to be descriptions of who or what a person is or might become. Immanuel, then, supposedly means God Among Us.

It does bother me, however, that a very large percent of the book deals with warnings and braggings and such... and the coming of the Messiah is briefly (almost passingly) mentioned in one sentence. It seems to me that this little tidbit of prophecy, possibly the greatest one of all time, might have had a correspondingly significant announcement and explanation laid out in such a way as to garner more attention. We are, as I understand it, supposed to "get it"... are we not? I did, in fact, nearly miss it... inundated as I was with the profound greatness and busyness and knowledge and mercy of God.

As a last comment, I guess I should explain my use of the word compelling earlier. If, as many Christians believe, Isaiah wrote the entire book, then the prophecy of the birth of Jesus (or Immanuel) is indeed compelling... even astounding. Citing differences in style and content, Bible scholars suspect there were as many as three authors of the book. If this is the case... and it isn't so hard to accept that church enthusiasts might have assembled supportive material as they deemed appropriate for their agenda... then one would have to suspect the entire Bible of similar contrivances. That aside, Isaiah 7:14 is the very first passage in the Old Testament that is compelling enough to me (assuming Isaiah wrote it) that it can be logged onto the side of the score sheet deemed "pro". There are many "cons", but I fully expected the Old Testament to be that way.

May 20, 2013... Spiritual Respectability, Acceptability, and Disability

I was wondering, this morning, about how my spiritual search will end... if indeed it does end. I have expressed that I have a great desire to find a valid path for my intangible existence to progress towards. What exactly does that mean, though? Will I become a "saved" Christian? ...or spurned atheist? Will I stumble onto an unexpected path that is completely beyond my sadly lacking foresight? As much as I think I need spirituality, is it really necessary, essential, or meaningful at all? Is it possible that the intangible side of me (or us) that I suspect is there, isn't? Am I wasting my time?

Gods have come and gone over the past several millennia. The Norse gods, however, accepted they were at one time, sort of disappeared and became the stuff of comic books. The ancient Greek and Roman Gods, likewise, fizzled into laughable legends and box office wonders. The Egyptian God Ra became blah. There seems to be no end to the truly magnificent deities that apparently turned out to be passing phases. Some lived in the limelight for centuries; some didn't. Most are relegated to a mythical realm that we modern thinkers recognize as the misguided and ignorant creations of…well…us.

Believers (of any faith) tend to consider their chosen faith as the correct one. That is why they are called believers, no doubt. I wonder, though, if a couple of thousand years from now comic books will feature Jesus as a superhero on the order of Thor or Hercules. Will this entire mess of religions dwindle away to obscurity as others have? If time is a consideration in how valid a religion is, perhaps we all should reconsider Hinduism since it predates Christian dogma by thousands of years… and is the third-largest religion in the world today after all of that time. Are we nothing more than misguided and gullible creatures of unending trial and error? Are these deities of the past and present, in reality, the same God… misunderstood enough to appear different to different peoples during different times? Then what about the societies that worshiped several Gods? We laugh at their ignorance, but religious wars of the past have proven that their beliefs are (or have been) valid enough to kill for.

What, I wonder, constitutes respectability regarding a particular faith? What makes a belief valid? …a certain number of adherents, maybe? …a measure of time in the limelight? …the level of risk involved in NOT believing? …how much money or power a particular religion has accumulated? What do I mean by spiritual disability? If there is such a thing, I mean it to be the apparent absence or deficiency of spiritual belief. In other words…what I have. My spiritual disability has become so noticeable and intolerable in my life that I have undertaken this rather imposing quest for intangible relief. I fear, though, that it may lead nowhere. I will definitely need more than self-validating manuscripts… and passionate urgings from others, to find my way. There may have been a time when I might have accepted a faith simply because "It says so here!"… but this is not that time. There may have been a time when the passions exuded by those close to me would rub off on me… but this is not that time. I am not blind. I am not all THAT stupid.

And I will not accept weak evidence or passionate hearsay regarding something as important as the salvation of my soul and the overdue contentment of my mind. Because of that promise to myself, this search for spiritual validity will continue.

May 24, 2013... The Salvation Equation

As I was writing the previous paragraph, I realized that I had inadvertently stumbled upon a curious idea that I really had not thought much about prior to this. I have always placed the idea of salvation into the same bag of slippery curiosities as several other subjects that I probably wouldn't consider someday. I have, however, made several references to my personal salvation in earlier discussions. It might be time, therefore, to examine, as best I can, just what salvation might mean... or if it really has a meaning at all.

It is probably the case that people often use words and ideas that they haven't really thought that much about... and I think I am guilty of that very thing, although it is likely more of an idiosyncrasy than a fault. What is probably worse, is that I probably convinced myself that I knew the meaning of the word (salvation), when I actually never investigated it at all. So...first...here is a definition from an online dictionary: Salvation (in the context of religion): "deliverance from sin and from the penalties of sin; redemption." In the interest of understanding, I will attempt to paraphrase. Assuming that sin is something we shouldn't do... and assuming that we all do it, salvation would mean that there is a way to absolve ourselves of our wrongdoings in the hope of attaining some sort of eternal peace... or avoiding some sort of damnation or judgment.

Obviously, as with much of what else I have written in this journal of mine, none of this has been studied by me in any official or sanctioned way. There have been no previous discussions of it with others. The idea here is to simply lay out my thoughts as they happen... and then go where they take me in an effort to harvest a tidbit or two of ingredients that will eventually mix up happily into a spiritual soup that is both palatable and healthy for me.

So (again)...what is salvation? It is obviously a commonly tossed-around word in the Bible. I would like to step back a bit, though, and think about whether or not salvation is real, whether it is attainable or not, and whether I should care at all.

From the perspective of an atheist, I should think that (spiritual) salvation would be a little perplexing... if not irrelevant. Why would one need or want to be delivered from sin if there is no judgment of sin? What flavor of morality one lived by would have to be some kind of personal decision... and not the concern of a deity.

A Christian believer, obviously, has the great Guidebook to follow regarding sin, its manifestations, and its redemption. But what about folks like me? How does an agnostic look at sin and salvation? Since there are many kinds of agnostics, there would seem to be many kinds of sin... and therefore a continuum of salvations, as well. As an agnostic theist, I accept that a God creator is as possible as any other creation idea. I, therefore, cannot discount a God from the salvation equation. The kind of God, however, is where things get complicated. If I was to lean toward the Christian believer's end of the agnostic spectrum, I would have to consider that God knows me and has a concern for my actions and spirit. In that instance, I would have to be concerned that my morality was in line with His... and that I lived in a manner that took His judgment into account with everything I did. If, however, I believed that there very well could be a deity that doesn't know me or keep track of anything I do, then (like the atheist) my sins would be determined by my own morality and my willingness to self regulate. I might also find forgiveness something that I administer to myself... in lieu of no caring greater power. Redemption... or salvation, would then be a matter of self-endowed benevolence... or more likely...something related to justification.

In all honesty, having a bit of Christian experience while young, I can say that I have adopted much of the Christian morality as my lifestyle of choice... whether or not there is a valid reason for doing it. Like most people, I like what I consider to be "good", and I tend to avoid what I consider to be "not good". What I consider, though, does not stray far from Biblical doctrine. If I wasn't so "open-minded", I would probably make a fine Christian... or at the very least, one that appears pious.

What salvation is…is interesting enough, but there are at least two other interesting facets of it that merit some thought. One is whether it is possible or not… and the other is whether it matters. First, then, regarding its possibility… I am thinking that it is partly a matter of how much of a believer one happens to be. Christians often refer to themselves as having been saved. Salvation, then, is the process whereby one becomes saved. And if I understand the principal… believe and you are automatically saved. As an agnostic, though, I wonder if there is a sort of salvation for those of us who have trouble with the swallowing of the entire Christian doctrine hook, line, and sinker. What if (…just a possibility…remember) there is not a God, or what if He is simply some entity that resides in another dimension that we lowly humans have only an inkling of? What if He caused the big bang for our universe as part of a multi-verse project and doesn't care in the least that a bunch of arrogant humans evolved to believe that they are somehow favored in ONE universe consisting of hundreds of billions of galaxies… each with hundreds of millions (or billions) of stars… many (or most) of which have at least one, and probably more, planets revolving around them? Let's face it; life happened on earth. If God meant for intelligent (hmmm!) humans to be the only… and chosen… lifeforms to deal with on our tiny, tiny, tiny speck of a world, why did He create an unimaginably huge universe (…and possibly others) when our wherewithal and lifespans are simply not big enough to see much of it. He quite obviously did not create the universe for our benefit, so it had to be for His own benefit… or the benefit of other lifeforms elsewhere… assuming, of course, that He created it at all.

Another point regarding the possibility of salvation is that WE humans seem to think that WE are somehow offered this seemingly wonderful redemptive afterlife… when the only indications that it is possible at all comes from our own writings, imaginings, voices in our heads, or whatever.

My point with all this is that WE (some of us) believe that there is a God who played a part in our existence. We (humans) documented what we call scripture and prophecy. WE interpret our own documentation to promote the meaning WE have on our sacred agendas, and WE are willing to kill and die for these ideas… none of which were actually, and directly, presented to us by a proven God entity.

Salvation, therefore, seems to me to be just one more of our possible perplexing inventions... interpreted to sound important and relevant and desirable, but which is unsubstantiated as a real spiritual possibility and which no one... not even God, has validated as anything more than a hopeful human invention. Blasphemy? Prove it.

June 5, 2013... The Great and Powerful...

I remember the Wizard of Oz scene in which the protagonists shudder in fear at the loud and pompous and empty ravings of the little man behind the curtain. The great and powerful Oz turned out to be the self-marketed invention of an unfortunate and all-too-human man... making the best of his situation. I wonder, now, if the film was at least a partial metaphor for the Old Testament. The resemblance is uncanny.

The Book of Jeremiah, in all honesty, is a preposterously long and tedious and confusing lesson on how to properly and completely threaten an obviously misguided group of hapless chosen ones... and their oppressors. Once again, the chosen ones have managed to motivate the (self-proclaimed) great and powerful God into anger, unending threats and revenge (...the hallmarks of a merciful and forgiving God?). Their "iniquities"... though bestowed upon them by You Know Who... are, again, an unbearable and intolerable thorn in God's side. He, therefore, arranges for the Babylonians to besiege and conquer the people of Judah and Jerusalem... whisk them off to Babylon, and enslave them for seventy years... after which, He changes His mind and decides to exact revenge on Babylon for doing His work. There is no shortage of angry exhortations, fearful threats and exhaustive ravings... as if this sort of thing worked in the past. Jeremiah, the official spokesman for God, somehow passes on the terrible message to everyone concerned and inexplicably lives through it all... in a time when don't kill the messenger seemingly had no meaning to anyone.

The book seems to be both, historic and prophetic. Although it is a bit confusing to me exactly what order things should be in. According to Jeremiah's writings,

God, himself, appears to talk in the past tense in places... if I understood it correctly. So God's prophecies to Jeremiah are sometimes a matter of what will be, and sometimes what has been. In fact, in my eyes, the prophetic history seems to be a bit too detailed... considering that previous prophecies by other prophets were considerably less detailed and, in fact, open to much interpretation. Now... two thousand years later, it looks to me like the prophecies could easily have been written AFTER the events they foretold... and conveniently interpreted to appear prophetic to further the agenda of the church. No doubt, though, Biblical scholars could show "evidence" to the contrary.

Another possibility is that the prophecies are indeed prophetic and what seems like logical explanations or likely speculation to me might very well be the true and accurate words of the Lord (through Jeremiah). Though a most fervent and probably incurable skeptic, even I have to live with my own prior convictions regarding possibilities. If I cannot prove the prophecies were faked (and I can't), then neither they (the prophecies) nor my own feelings regarding them can be discounted. One is as possible as the other...lacking further evidence.

My considered judgment, then, is that the Book of Jeremiah either is or is not valid prophecy.

June 7, 2013... The Validity of Lamentations

Jeremiah was apparently a citizen of Jerusalem... as far as I can discern. It is, therefore, not surprising that he would lament the destruction of his hometown... or is it? As the prophet of Jerusalem's destruction, he obviously knew it would be destroyed according to the word of God... and supposedly well before it happened. Although it is understandable that he would suffer the loss of it, he surely knew better than anyone that the Lord made it His work... for His own justified reason, and for His revengeful purpose. He also knew that it was temporary work. After 70 years the chosen ones would be redeemed and return to Jerusalem to rebuild it and re-populate it. The Babylonians would be properly dealt with and all would be well...with time.

Jeremiah was a faithful believer in God. He never questioned God's wisdom. Why, then, would he lament so much the fulfillment of his own prophesies when he wholeheartedly supported God and His works. I will grant that he was human. The city was not only rock walls and evil-doers. There was, no doubt, much to miss in the total destruction... justified or not. I wonder, though, why the assemblers of the Bible chose to include a Book of Lamentations. Wasn't the justified destruction of Jerusalem by the Lord valid enough for our story? Did we have some psychological need to demonstrate the emotional trauma that it caused, as well? Perhaps Jeremiah's own lamenting would somehow inspire future generations to respect the will of God to a greater degree. Personally, I found the idea that Jeremiah found God to be both merciful and revengeful as a perplexing dichotomy. The chosen women in Jerusalem supposedly ate their own chosen children. One can only assume that the evil children deserved to be eaten by their parents. Why else would God sacrifice innocent young chosen ones in an effort to punish the iniquities of their chosen elders?

June 11, 2013... A Prophet and Loss Statement

My experiences with the Bible to date have left me feeling somewhat lacking in spiritual progress. I sincerely hope this won't continue as a trend while I muddle through the Great Book... especially due to the fact that it is of such great importance in the Christian world these days... not to mention days past. The local church that I have been attending for the past year or so openly disregards the Old Testament... interpreting the New Testament as a new covenant that leaves the old one no longer valid. They (the pastors) do, however... from time to time, quote from it... as suits their whims. This is something I find curious and a bit disconcerting. They (the pastors) also talk often of prophecy and seem to encourage churchgoers to recognize or practice a sort of personal dialog with God... one which goes beyond prayer. On a weekly basis, people will stand up and tell how they have suffered some sort of misfortune or malady, prayed for deliverance, and when things worked out one way or another, attributed it to their personal connection with the Almighty. It seems there are no positive results that can be attained by human initiative alone. There is no such thing as coincidence. Faith appears to make every situation a planned one, every mystery an essential part of God's way, every good thing His work, and every bad thing the Devil's work. I suppose it makes everything easier to accept or reconcile when true understanding fails.

I find, though, that my skepticism and curiosity, and critical thinking are precious to me... whether they get in the way of instant explanations or not. I simply cannot allow myself to encounter a situation that compels me to attribute what transpires as the work of some imagined entity... with nothing whatsoever to substantiate it... other than the eons-old writings of self-proclaimed chosen ones or prophets. The key word here is "self-proclaimed". God did not announce to the world that Jeremiah or Ezekiel would be His spokesmen. They announced it themselves. It is written over and over that, "so sayeth the Lord God". I should think that a God capable of selecting and blessing a "son of man" with the sacred and all-important word of God would simply and openly substantiate His chosen prophet... rather than relying on the manifestations of their prophecies to convince an admittedly stiff-necked people to swallow the unusual and mysterious ways of the unseen entity. It looks to me that God, for some strange and incalculable reason, just doesn't like to take the direct approach to anything. He doesn't just speak directly to everyone to be done with it. He doesn't simply make things work... as a God should certainly be able to do. He doesn't like how things work out sometimes... and gets mad, when any self-respecting God should be able to control His temper and NOT make mistakes. He wouldn't create a troublesome people and then become frustrated by their trouble. He might explain, exactly, just why a prophet is necessary in the first place.

The Book of Ezekiel, like Jeremiah, is a lengthy, exhaustive blame and threats tirade. There seem to be many similarities... not that a comparison is called for. What I find most curious, though, is that both Jeremiah and Ezekiel lived during the same time and in the same place. They prophesy similar Godly anger, threats of doom, and future events. Unless I am mistaken, though, there is no mention of Ezekiel in Jeremiah, and no mention of Jeremiah in Ezekiel. Did God forget that He already had a prophet and contact another? Were Jeremiah and Ezekiel on opposite sides of the street preaching the same message at the same time to the same people? Why didn't Jeremiah have to cook his meat using cow dung for fuel?

Through Ezekiel, God mentions a few times that certain unfortunates would "go down into Hell". Again, unless I am mistaken, there has been no prior mention of Hell in the Bible at all. I wonder how Ezekiel... or anyone else for that matter... might possibly know what Hell was supposed to be. I certainly have no recollection of it ever being explained before this... and I really can't say that it is explained in Ezekiel either. ...just mentioned... that's all. No doubt, there are references to Hell in other manuscripts, but it seems rather odd to me that something as vitally important as this repository for lost or forsaken souls (...as far as I know) is barely mentioned in the Bible... and not explained in the least. He might as well have threatened to send the recipients of His anger to the Andromeda Galaxy. With no explanation or apparent understanding of what Hell is, how could anyone have been intimidated by the prospect of going there? Very odd, indeed.

One last observation regarding the Book of Ezekiel. Once God finished with his seemingly endless tirade of threats and punishments, He whisked Ezekiel off to instruct him how to rebuild the chosen one's new city, apportion the land surrounding it for the twelve families of Israel, and how to rebuild the temple in which the Lord intended to live... and indeed, inhabited immediately. There was also a considerable lesson on how and when to perform ritual sacrifices, who would do what in and around the temple, and how to make a new river... apparently with salt water and ocean fishes in it...complete with new trees on its banks. I have to admit, though, that despite the numerous mentions of "the prince", I really could not discern who, exactly, He was referring to. I seem to remember God saying earlier that Isreal would be presided over by kings of David's lineage. I have no memory of any princes in the neighborhood. My memory, though... such as it is, is another creation of God's... as I understand it, although I have not encountered anything in the Bible so far that indicates how or why we unchosen ones got here, what purpose WE might have on this earth, or whether or not we might, at some point, become somewhat chosen... or included in the same promise of salvation, or find some sacred inheritances, or even aspire to an eternal heaven. Hopefully, I will acquire... as Steve Martin so misunderstandingly put it in The Jerk... a special purpose.

June 21, 2013... Oh Danny Boy

The Book of Daniel has turned out to be somewhat of a surprise to me. It was perplexing enough to discover that Jeremiah and Ezekiel lived at around the same time and in the same place... without apparent knowledge of each other, despite the "fact" that they both claimed an intimate and exclusive discourse with God. Now I find that a third prophet also is a contemporary of the time. Daniel, too, is chosen by the Almighty as a spokesman and a favored one among the favored ones. He, too, seems to be unaware of the other prophets as there is absolutely no mention of the others in the Book of Daniel. Although I am making every attempt to find validity in... and an understanding of... the Bible, the Book itself is hindering my quest for spirituality. It simply doesn't appear to be the handbook for living that I expected or hoped for. I admit that I am unqualified to criticize the Bible in any serious way, but it was written/assembled to be a helpful guide for common people... if I understand its purpose. So far, in my humble opinion, it is neither helpful nor a guide. It is a confusing mess of ridiculous, incredible, and quite unbelievable tales. I have to believe that it is "based on a true story", but it leaves me with more questions and more uncertainty than I think it should.

...and this brings me to my most contentious point about Daniel. The Book includes its own interpretations... supposedly to clarify the words of God, but unfortunately...the interpretations seem to need interpreting too. Once again, God missed His opportunity to clearly and unequivocally communicate to the masses... His warnings, wishes, concerns, and plans. Instead, He sends angels... that look like men... to describe kings and princes... that look like fantastical beasts to explain in uncertain terms a future that is either inevitable, possible, or laughable. I should think that a prophecy regarding the end of all things might be important enough to speak clearly about. No parables. No guesswork. No interpretations. No doubts or confusion. Would it be so difficult for the creator of the universe to simply say, "You're all going to die... next week on Wednesday at 3:15 pm."?

I wonder how many sidewalk prophets walking around with two-sided placards announcing the end of the world might actually be the legitimate and official spokespersons of the Almighty. If the God of the universe truly wants us, lowly humans to amount to something worthy of His lofty consideration, why would He not simply pop out of His cloud, allay our fears, demonstrate His reality, clearly speak His message and be on His way... without all the blood sprinkling, purple robes, gold accoutrements, goat killings, idol silliness, monsters, proxy prophets...and all the rest? If ever there was a reason to become an atheist, the Bible appears to be it...so far.

June 29, 2013... A Digression of Prophets

It is with a certain dismay and regret that I admit I have begun to tire of the prophets... or the idea of prophets. Since the various Books of the prophets take up so much of the Bible, I would think their significance or messages might impress upon me how important they are in the entire story of God. On the contrary, I have found them a silly distraction. If ever there was a human being who might stir the anger of God, it is probably me, but then... I am not among the fortunate chosen ones. I am, therefore, perhaps, beneath the notice of the Almighty... quest for spirituality or not. The prophets, though, just do not impress me. They smack of sidewalk Armageddon hawkers who would promptly be arrested for vagrancy or institutionalized these days.

Now, with the Book of Hosea, the Bible backtracks a couple of centuries and, once again, reiterates the previous warnings against idols and "harlotry" and so forth. The wise and noble scholars who assembled the Books of the Bible apparently found the major prophets lacking in their ability to properly influence a potential reader... and so added a handful of "minor" prophets for good measure. And now that I finally believed myself past the story of the fall of Jerusalem and the severe reprimand of the Jewish chosen ones, I am now once again obliged to endure another onslaught of Godly warnings and threats.

It is my general opinion that an almighty God really should be able to communicate His wishes to His people in an efficient and very clear manner... without the arguably stupid reliance on myriad sidewalk prophets who preach an unending litany of doom and gloom over the course of (literally) centuries. I realize that the Almighty supposedly moves in mysterious ways, but it seems ridiculous that He would operate in such a roundabout and indirect way to advance His agenda when He... according to His own claims... is perfectly capable of snapping His sacred fingers to make things instantly acceptable. When He doesn't get His way, He throws a temper tantrum and (through his proxies) threatens His own chosen ones with disaster while all the while proclaiming Himself a merciful God.

And so...if I understand things correctly, God created the chosen ones... and the unchosen ones, as well. He gave them instructions regarding how to be worthy of His choice. He also made them not only capable of sin but also likely to sin repeatedly. Then He becomes angry with them when they do exactly what He made them to do. He bellows His rage, warnings, and threats to proxy spokesmen (no women) who He, Himself, apparently made quite ineffective since He is relegated to use several prophets over the course of centuries to make His point... some of which operated at the same time, in the same place, and preached the same message to the same people... with seemingly no knowledge of the other legitimate prophets.

What is, perhaps, most distressing to me... as I slog through this Old Testament, besides the fact that there IS an Old Testament for some reason, is that a fairly large segment of the world's population actually takes these Books seriously... and is willing to kill to prove it. While it is most sincerely true that I admittedly harbor biases and ignorance... and am probably not informed enough about what I am reading to be of serious concern to any "true" believer. I do, however, consider myself reasonably educated, passably sensible, and a critical enough thinker to recognize debatable validity when I see it.

July 1, 2013... Joel, Amos & Obadiah

The three Books named above are quite short, quite similar, and nothing new in my eyes, and since I have already made my opinions about the minor prophets evident, there is no real need to comment on them to any significant degree. I will simply say that it struck me in Joel (2:12-13) when God pronounces, "Now return to the LORD your God, For He is gracious and compassionate, Slow to anger, abounding in lovingkindness And relenting of evil". I can only reiterate that after many Books and chapters of vehement threats of doom and gloom, for God to proclaim Himself gracious and compassionate, slow to anger and abounding in lovingkindness... there has been precious little of those very things to validate His claims. He has made it quite clear to me that He is simply (at this point in the Bible) NOT what He seems to think He is. Perhaps with the inclusion of even more minor prophets, these claims might be substantiated, but I am simply not seeing it. I will assert, however...again...that I am not a Bible scholar and I do not possess the knowledge or credentials to go up against the Great Book... or even its components... with arguments that can compete with two centuries worth of very comprehensive study by countless men of nearly universally accepted learning and well-reasoned interpretations. Despite my obvious dislike of faith being the basis for validity, it is difficult for me to dispute the Biblical work that greater men than I have accomplished. I see no reason, however, to discount my own ignorance, my own sincere attempt to remedy it, or my personal musings in doing so... simply because others do not happen to share my skepticism or willingness to find a way through this convoluted and ridiculously interpreted text. Though I make mistakes, I am thinking about my intangible existence... its origin, its reason for being... if there is one, and its fate. How can this possibly be a wrong move? I have every hope that through my personal investigations and discussions, I will find something that will compel me to validate a faith that makes sense to me. I cannot, and will not, accept pleadings or pressure from others as reason enough to believe a certain way. This is not a decision I take lightly. Others, likewise, will not accept my skepticism as an influence on them. In this, we have something in common.

July 2, 2013... Concerning My Raison D'etre

After the last discussion, I began thinking about the reason for my soul's existence... or whether there IS a reason... or whether there should be. It probably goes without saying that any discussion regarding such a thing... with myself or other-

wise... will most likely be fruitless in light of the intangible nature of my consciousness. It is interesting, though, to ponder not only what my intangible existence is,
and where it might have come from, but also why. Why am I here? ...oh, not my
physical self, obviously, although that is another point of contention, but my intangible existence. WHY am I here?

Guesses and thoughtful intelligent reasonings abound, but the age-old question
really is unanswered... utterly. Those of a pious nature will often proclaim with
confidence that only God can know, or that we are here to serve God...or to serve
each other. Rod Serling's classic tale of aliens visiting earth..."To Serve Man" notwithstanding, I find myself asking not only if there is a reason, but if there should
be one. If I boil the question down a bit, it only gets more interesting: Why am I
sentient? Why do I ask why?

The question of whether there should be a reason for my soul is arguably as
interesting as why it exists in the first place. We humans have a natural tendency
to want answers for our questions, but does our inquisitive nature really have to
go beyond our evolved survival instinct? It is easy enough to see that when we
strive to understand why it becomes necessary to run from a teased bull, we can
probably exist somewhat longer than our stupidity might otherwise allow. But why
does it matter if we become interested in what lies beyond what we can see through
a telescope thirteen billion light-years from the Earth? Why does Jupiter have over
70 moons? How do things like this have anything whatsoever to do with the possibility of a God when they were not even known a hundred years ago? Why do I
have questions? Why do questions exist? Why do I care? Why should I care?

It occurs to me that despite the tendency for us to want answers, and to make
speculative explanations, we really usually only guess... at least when it concerns
the intangible things that we all appreciate as real. God IS a possibility. I
acknowledge that. The possibility is entirely as possible as that there is NO God.
This is why I consider myself an agnostic theist. In the absence of other viable
reasons for my existence, I am compelled to at least partially accept the one possible
reason that HAS been put forth... and accepted by perhaps a billion people on this
planet. Until I encounter a better explanation than the one I have so far, I will

grudgingly and limitedly accept God as my possible creator...for the time being. Why? ...because I have nothing else to work with at this point.

In a curious way, I am ashamed of my last statement. I might even admit that I am ashamed for the entire human race... that despite our blatant exultations of accomplishments, we do not seem to be any closer to answering the question, "Why are we here?" than we ever have been. As for whether or not we should exist, it appears to me to be a question of whether we accept the concept of randomness or coincidence, or luck. My wife would probably say that we are here because God designed things that way... whether we understand or not. My answer would have to be, "Which rule book did that come from?" As time goes by, I find myself repeating the same questions to myself: How can anyone expect anyone to believe claims that cannot be substantiated? How can anyone even assume the righteousness of making such claims? If someone has the (God-given?) human capability to make these claims with self-righteous abandon, wouldn't the designated recipient of the claim also have an equally valid, God-given, right to skepticism with which to challenge it? Is belief or faith somehow correct behavior and skepticism or disbelief not? ...are they both not God-given... and therefore valid?

As I almost promised, I do not have any more answers than anyone else... even after putting a bit of thought into it. I DO happen to believe in randomness. I DO accept coincidences...and even luck... despite the fact that I don't know what luck is exactly. I do know, though, that if I somehow am able to glean a bit of spirituality from these personal probings and my Biblical explorations, I will consider myself lucky. What I fear...is that after all of this work, and all of this thought, and all my vague excuses to my wife, I may not find what I am looking for at all. At this point in my studies, I'm afraid it looks to be going that way. I most sincerely hope I am wrong.

July 8, 2013... A Small Reprise of the Pentateuch

If I was to characterize the first books of the Bible in some simple and probably thoughtless way, it would likely end up something like this: an interesting, but wildly imaginative series of unbelievable tales. As umpire Jim Odom said, "I call them like I see them."

The Book of Jonah, as far as I am concerned, is a throwback to the Pentateuch tales. In fact, it almost seems out of place in the midst of later books that rave about sin and Godly revenge and doom and gloom. I had been wondering where the story of Jonah... and what I had thought was a whale... would occur in the Bible. I was, in fact, running out of Old Testament. Since I had not read the Bible previous to this endeavor, I was not aware that the Book of Jonah existed at all. So it was that when I came upon the Book of Jonah, I was anticipating a lively story... having been somewhat familiar with it from my hapless exposure to religion when I was young.

Although considered a "lesser" prophet, Jonah seems to have been one of the more adept at prophecy. Even the great prophets, like Moses for instance, had a difficult time convincing people that God was working through him. It took what we call miracles to lend credence to the prophet's words. Even then, the chosen ones disregarded the covenant repeatedly... despite warnings and punishments. In fact, none of the prophets before Jonah was able to convincingly influence the people to realign their priorities with God with any permanent success. Jonah, though, convinced the 120,000 inhabitants of Nineveh to do just that... with no exceptions. This is keeping in mind that Nineveh was a large city in Assyria... not Israel. These were the enemies of the chosen ones...and Jonah was able to convince them to change their ways and accept God. Interesting.

One point of amusement... After Jonah delivers his message and God reconsiders His doom for Nineveh, Jonah gets angry with the Almighty... supposedly for sending him to prophesy God's doom, and then pardoning the Ninevites. Jonah simply didn't think the whole thing was right. As I understand it, though, Nineveh was utterly destroyed a short time later anyway. So, God apparently reneged on His own forgiveness and totally wiped Nineveh off the map permanently.

There is also the matter of the big fish. Is this the best God could do? ...or is it possible the writings of Jonah were somewhat on the imaginative side? When I think about it, Jonah relayed his story of what happened to him in what is now known as the Book of Jonah. I wonder…if I was to write a narrative about a conversation with God, then describe how I was swallowed by a big fish for three days until I agreed to do His bidding… I have no doubts that I would soon find myself in reasoned residence at the nearest asylum. My story, however, would certainly eventually attain a lofty significance worthy of Biblical publication.

I have said several times in the past that if I was to somehow encounter the Almighty… after having lived a fairly turbulent and regrettable life, I would surely and most vigorously have words with Him. Jonah seems to be the only human being (that I know of) who actually did exactly that. God managed to appease him, but I find it quite amusing that lowly Jonah got mad at God… and got away with it. That, in my humble opinion, is one considerable goal for my bucket list. My offer still holds.

July 10, 2013… More of the Same

Although I have little to say about the Books of Micah and Nahum, considering that they are once again more of the same… threats and doom, I will mention again, that Micah wrote his prophecies during the same time Isaiah did. So, once again, there are two prophets in the same area, relaying the same words of God to the same people about similar doom and redemption… and without the apparent knowledge of each other, despite the fact that the same God is working through them both. Once again, there is mention of a "ruler" who will arise from Bethlehem… one who comes from the time of "everlasting" (?). I might ask…when is the time of everlasting? Why am I not told in proper plain language that a Messiah will be sent to the world of man… from God, on behalf of God, and for what purpose? So much is nearly always left to interpretation.

That said, it is interesting that Micah predicts the coming of someone who will be a ruler of peace. Skeptic or not, it is difficult for me to guess that this "ruler" is anyone other than Jesus Christ. If the prophecy did indeed occur as noted… hundreds of years before Christ, then it is compelling information that lends credence to the viability of God. This is, I have to think, one of the tipping points that convinced C.S. Lewis to relax his skepticism and allow the fingers of faith to begin their work on him.

Unfortunately, I can only describe Nahum as ho-hum…more of the same.

July 19, 2013… More and More of the Same… and… Here Come 'da Judge

Habakkuk, a supposed contemporary of Jeremiah, Nahum, and Zephaniah, again prophesied a similar message about the coming of Babylon and the fall of Jerusalem. He and Zephaniah preached about the wisdom of having faith and rejoicing in the Lord. It also suddenly becomes a concern that other nations of the world are under the jurisdiction of God. The locals are now told that God can command a foreign army to come and destroy them… or send a local one to destroy the foreigners. I wonder, though, if God turned a blind eye to China…or Peru…or South Dakota.

Haggai, so far as I can discern, was appointed prophet in Jerusalem after the return of the chosen ones from Babylon. His mandate (from God) was to nudge the people into rebuilding the temple. Zechariah, likewise, talks about the "day of the Lord" as a not-so-subtle hint of the apocalypse, I assume. This has always been a bit of a mystery to me in all honesty. Nearly two thirds of the Bible is the story of the chosen ones, their trials and tribulations and failings and redemption. Although I haven't progressed into the New Testament yet, I believe, at this point, that it suddenly speaks to all people… not just the chosen ones. I will think about that when I encounter it, but my thought, for now, pertains to the idea of an apocalypse and judgment day. Although I am literally thinking about this as I write, a judgment day doesn't make any sense to me. Why should those of us who are not the chosen ones be judged for our inequities when up to this point in the Bible we were, in essence, ignored by God? As unchosen ones, the things we believed or did or didn't do didn't matter. All of a sudden we are told that we will be judged? Why? Why should I care? Blasphemy or not, it appears to me that God, Himself, suffers from inequities. He shows favoritism to one group of people for thousands of years… to the disadvantage, or dismissal, of all the other peoples on the planet, then comes up with this idea of judgment day for all. I wholeheartedly reject the whole business as stupid nonsense.

Malachi brings up the rear of the Old Testament. He preaches against divorce (which I, generally, agree with). He admonishes the contemporary priests for cheating in their sacrifices... and encourages a return to God and the covenant. All-in-all, more of the same.

July 20, 2013... Out With the Old, In With the New

As perplexing and convoluted as it appeared to me, the Old Testament is a reasonably interesting tale that is likely "based on a true story". Which parts of it are true are largely a matter of interpretation, and of course, faith. The fact that much, if not all, of it is based on ancient writings that date back to the approximate times of the events in the story lends a certain credibility to it, although we human beings have been notoriously and conspicuously wrong about so many things throughout our history that any significant beliefs based on these old stories can hardly be considered one hundred percent valid. Did we not believe the earth was flat for a time? Wasn't it considered sacred and unarguable church doctrine that the earth was the center of the universe? I'm sure Galileo and Copernicus would have something to say about this. Not so long ago, eggs were bad for us... and margarine was good.

I have encountered a great many people who hold solid opinions about the Bible (in general), despite the fact that they have never read it. I am loathe to admit that I was one of them. Essentially, the Bible has developed such a lofty and unarguable status that anyone who questions any part of it is looked upon as blasphemous and radically uninformed, atheist or even fair game for misfortune. Even the legitimate and sincere informed will likely suffer ridicule, at the very least, for the slightest mention of questionable interpretation regarding the Bible. God, Himself, at one time, would have trembled with rage with one such as me who questions His very existence and validity. These days... perhaps because of His intermediary, He is incommunicado.

I find it interesting that God could not rely on the heartfelt and often vocalized convictions of His own chosen people, but He will accept anyone, supposedly, on faith alone these days. As I have said, haven't we human beings proven in no uncertain way that we are not reliable in any way whatsoever... even for God, Himself?

Although I have not begun to delve into the New Testament at this point, I am looking forward to it with great anticipation and hope. In all honesty, the Old Testament, in my humble opinion, is a silly, convoluted, incredulous, perverted, and misinterpreted mess of a tale that God, Himself, must look upon as a very funny joke. We, however, despite our zealous "faith", happen to be the butts of it.

July 21, 2013... The Unfailing Failings of Us All

I mentioned earlier that my own relative failures as a person, over the course of fifty or so years, led to my search for personal identity, psychological redemption, and spiritual direction... the result of which has culminated in the writing of this manuscript. I admit my failings... all of them. I also repent them... that is, I apologize for them to whomever I may have affected in an adverse way over the years. This repentance... which I am quite serious about, is also directed to God... assuming I find enough validity in my searchings to accept His existence, His grace, and His salvation. He, likewise, would have to find me forgivable and tolerable. But when I consider my own personal deficiencies... and study them to the best of my abilities, I find, disturbingly, that many of the same "inequities" are found, to various degrees, in virtually everyone. Unfortunately, most of us are not aware of our own failings... or to what extent we have them. We seem to detect them in others... and even challenge them in what are usually unpleasant and detestable ways. But we do not seem to see the very same problems in ourselves... in fact, we usually vehemently deny, minimize or justify our own inequities. I have been guilty of these things, and since I became aware of it, I have found that everyone is guilty to some extent, as well.

The point of all this, if my verbal wanderings can be excused, is that God created us all (supposedly), in His own image (surprisingly), and with full knowledge of what He was doing (incredibly). God then, if I can extrapolate, has failings, too. He, Himself, finds that He has underestimated His own chosen people. He has expressed regret on more than one occasion for the results of His own work. He has altered His strategies in how He deals with these failures. He has even scrapped His own self-image from the "fear of God", fire and brimstone, Old Testament entity to the New Testament "love of God", a merciful and forgiving entity who specializes in redemption and salvation. So…it seems to be evident that we all have failings. The apple doesn't fall far from the tree. Like father like son.

July 22, 2013… A Coincidence of Birthdays

Today is my birthday. It is also the day I read about the birth of Christ in the Book of Matthew. Superstition might dictate that I see a significance in that, but I like to think of superstition as nonsense… and coincidences as entirely uncoincidental.

I think I have mentioned several times in prior writings that I have a sincere hope the New Testament will hold a promise of spiritual direction for me. I will, here and now, reiterate my dedication to finding it… with what I hope is an open mind, an honest heart, and a willingness to go where it leads…providing it does, indeed, lead me somewhere. I will, however, use the exact same built-in critical resources to examine my findings… that I used in the Old Testament. I don't mean to hint at a pessimistic approach… but I will call an aromatic deposit of excrement…a bunch of shit if, for all intents and purposes, it appears to be one.

I suppose it will come as no surprise, to any hapless reader of my thoughts, that I have found a point of contention on the very first page of Matthew. I had hoped for a more palatable introduction to the New Testament… and I still harbor hope that I will find considerably fewer troublesome details in it, but I will discuss this one point… as it has presented itself.

The very first words detail the genealogy of Joseph… from Abraham, through fourteen generations, to David, through fourteen more generations, to the Babylon exile, through another fourteen generations to Joseph. This is, no doubt, to indicate and emphasize that Jesus came from the chosen ones… what is now referred to as the Jews. There is no genealogy for Mary, mother of Jesus. So although the lineage of Joseph is established from the start... it can be assumed (...are we sure, though?) that Mary is also descended from the chosen ones. The problem, as I see it, concerns the specified "fact" that Joseph is not Jesus' father. Mary supposedly had a virgin birth. She was impregnated by the Holy Spirit... not Joseph. How then is the lineage of Joseph of any consequence? If the Book of Matthew had logged the lineage of Mary, I might have made the connection between Jesus and the Jews more easily. Joseph, essentially, married into the family. He raised Jesus as his own son, but in actuality was not his father at all. Now I must ask myself, "Was Jesus a Jew?" He is often referred to as the king of the Jews, but it is not established whether Mary was a Jew at all. Joseph, according to the scripture itself, is clearly NOT His father... his lineage doesn't count.

I don't mean to belittle, in any way, the significance of Jesus by this observation. I am merely trying to use the Great Book to glean whatever meaningful story I can, regarding Jesus, the Christian dogma, and how it might be of spiritual value to me. I don't believe I am interpreting anything incorrectly here. It plainly states in Matthew 1:18 that, "...before they came together, she was found with child of the Holy Ghost." And Matthew 1:20 states, "...that which is conceived in her is of the Holy Ghost." And finally, Matthew 1:25 says that Joseph, "...knew her not till she had brought forth her firstborn son...". Joseph is plainly confirmed as a Jew... but is not related by blood to Jesus at all. Mary is clearly mentioned as the mother, but not a confirmed Jew... therefore Jesus can only be assumed Jewish... another interpretation, once again.

From my (somewhat) humble and ignorant perspective, Matthew appears to be essentially an overview of the life of Jesus. Since I am not familiar with the structure of the New Testament... or the reasons for the way it was assembled... I will assume (forgive me), for now, that what follows will be embellishments of the story, other perspectives, corroboration and other details that will hopefully lend credence to an otherwise unlikely story. I might also elaborate a bit about just what I do accept, as an agnostic theist, about God and Jesus... at this early encounter with the New Testament. It will be interesting, and I hope... productive, to compare my current perspective with my post-New Testament one. I should probably have explained exactly where I draw my lines earlier in this journal of discovery.

Perhaps, had I thought of it, I would have. As it stands, I believe it can be summarized adequately in a paragraph or two.

With no other valid explanations for the existence of the universe (or its initial Big Bang), God... though entirely abstract... and certainly under-understood, is really the only viable possibility that has been put forth to us lowly humans for intellectual consideration. I do not accept that an absence of other explanations is a good enough reason to close the book and call the problem solved. Without any proof at all, I accept God as the only vigorously considered explanation possibility that has ever been presented to the human race. Science is wonderful, valid, and interesting... and I wholeheartedly support and accept it, but it has still been unable to even theorize WHY the universe is. Silly as it sounds to me, the Bible posits that the universe was essentially created by God for His own mysterious agenda. It can be considered quite certain that when a better... or even just another... reason is detailed and vigorously argued, I will be there to consider it. I do not believe that God knows me, or anyone else... at this point in my studies. I might very well be wrong... and I am quite willing to accept that upon validation, but I see no viable reason to base the existence or salvation of my soul (intangible existence) on a wild tale of unsubstantiated claims assembled into one Book by biased believers centuries ago. At this point, and with only the benefit of what I have encountered so far, I believe that life on earth is probably an accident... a result of some ancient, haphazard, nudge by God that likely went totally unnoticed by Him... if, indeed, He has the capability or desire to notice. These are the kind of words that will likely stir up great consternation for many others, but it should be remembered that I consider the God I acknowledge as the EXACT same God that the Bible talks about. I just don't accept the unsubstantiated and completely unlikely tales attributed to His story as anything other than the uninformed wishful thinking of an ancient, uneducated people who felt a need for...well...spiritual direction. I do, however, respect that the opinions and beliefs of others... however much they differ from mine, are equally as valid... since they (the others) have little more in the way of proofs to go on than I.

As for the story of Jesus... I'm afraid I must defer my final feelings regarding His existence and significance and validity, though I do have some thoughts going into my study. At this point... and it is quite early, I expect that Jesus will be shown to be a real person... with considerable historical record validating His existence. I actually do not expect to dispute his life on earth. His significance, likewise, cannot be argued. And there are two thousand years of acknowledgment by billions of people to verify His validity as an important figure in the story of God and man. For now, I will not comment further on Jesus the man... or even Jesus the Son of God. Instead, I would like to sort out and convey my thoughts on the general morality of Jesus if I can. It is this that I find fascinating and worthwhile and compelling.

Whether the entire story of Jesus is true or not, I find that it is most ingenious. He, Himself, seems to have had an answer for everything... if all the claims in Matthew are true. The very idea that one entity might draw the sins of all people onto Himself in order to purge the inequities from (or redeem) an imperfect people is quite profound and, I'll say it again...ingenious. It is the kind of idea that one might easily attribute to a God... or His proxy. It is the one thing in this convoluted and confusing story that has the power and appeal to attract the multitudes of the earth into a (somewhat) cohesive group of fellow believers. In all honesty, I really don't have a clear opinion of how this relates to me, personally. I hope to identify, consider and settle some of the details that make it a concern as I progress. What strikes me, though, is the fact that these same people who I previously called "uninformed" and "uneducated" either came up with this singular redemption idea on their own somehow... as a justification for, and escape from, their sins... or it was handed to them...by Jesus. Either way, the problem of how to reconcile their own historically documented sins and inequities seems to get dealt with in one fell swoop. Amazing. Either these ancient people were considerably more inventive and capable than I imagined, or the story of Jesus, as presented by Matthew, is valid. Since I have a somewhat negatively-charged and limited view of the virtues demonstrated by human beings, the possibilities that the story of Jesus leaves with me are, to say the least, intriguing.

July 28, 2013... Mark My Words

Although I have seldom been shown to be right about many things, it appears that I may have been at least marginally correct about what follows Matthew in the Bible. The Book of Mark... when compared to Matthew, might easily be seen as...the same thing only different. ...a rewrite of the same story... by someone else. I suppose the reasons for the rewrite are somewhat obvious... reinforcement by repetition of an otherwise somewhat questionable story.

It occurs to me that the story of Jesus, being the incredible improbability that it is, might be considerably more acceptable to the masses if it is told in similar detail by separate sources. The standard police investigative model uses the questioning of several witnesses to develop a credible case for both, the prosecution and the defense. The pro-Son of God camp, then, does just that... by virtue of several eye-witness accounts, establishes the validity of the Son of God story. And despite my probably belittling observations, I do acknowledge the legitimacy of this technique... whether in finding a legal precedent or establishing the legitimacy of the deity in question. Does this mean God is real, or that Jesus was of sacred descent? Who am I to decide such a thing? Then again...who am I to presume that I am qualified to even entertain the possibility? I guess I have to think I am as qualified as any of the "multitudes" who also consider the Bible in church or their individual hearts. I am not so different than the poor of the masses who Jesus encountered in His travels. I am ignorant, I doubt, I have sinned, I yearn for redemption. I can say, though, with a sincere certainty, that a miracle here and there would help considerably. It is a simple thing to open a Book purported to be assembled from two-thousand-year-old manuscripts and read about unbelievable miracles that happened quite frequently. But where are these miracles now? Why are all the unbelievables in the distant and inaccessible and unverifiable past? It seems entirely too convenient for proponents of miracles to preach faith as the only way to accept these unlikely events. If the people of Jesus' time were deserving of these proofs, why not us in these subsequent modern times? Are we any less gullible or ignorant? Are we somehow more likely to believe than those who allegedly saw miracles firsthand? Are my doubts and concerns somehow less deserving of similar demonstrations of sacred legitimacy? Will I go to Hell because God created me to ask these questions... and not simply accept Him with only the unverifiable two-thousand-year-old stories to go on? If I am expected (by God) to have faith in Him unconditionally, why then did He create me to need a measure of evidence for acceptance to take hold? Did He not create skepticism itself? Can I be faulted for practicing the very skepticism He graced me with? What kind of "test" is that?

July 29, 2013... I'm Just Saying...

A thought occurred to me today. (There are those who would aim their incredulous smile towards me at that.) I was driving home for lunch when I suddenly realized that my own death... which will come soon enough... will not be entirely without some appeal to me. This may seem like the irrational blurt of an unstable soul, but I will make an effort to unravel it for myself... as well as any hapless reader. Sometimes, my writing serves as my thinking. This is such a time.

Like most people I suppose, I have experienced a more than adequate amount of misfortune and grief, and stress in my life. There are times, even now, when my "inequities" catch up with me and nip relentlessly at my heels. Sometimes I conjure them myself, and at other times they are perhaps thoughtlessly picked up by others and whipped at me like a curled up towel in the hands of a bully. I mentioned earlier that I repent, with all my heart, the unfortunate duress my past ignorance inflicted on others. It was, alas, much too late in my life that I became aware of my own shortcomings... and began to address them. Many others, though, have not discovered theirs... much to my own dismay and frustration. What I see in me, I see in them. What I have tried to work on in me, I have no jurisdiction over in them. The inability to quell their sufferings... or the effects of it on others, is quite disheartening. It has been a decade of realization for me... with a full measure of disappointment... that these things will always be there for others and for me. I am weary of it...very weary. I am beginning to understand how the elderly eventually give up on life and simply pass.

I am not, however, bringing this up to depress myself or others. Since this frustrating inability to "fix" things is chronic, I began wondering about the spiritual potential for an acceptance of God and/or Jesus to remedy my yearnings for peace.

No doubt, it was similar feelings of helplessness and hopelessness that made a great number of people, past and present, more willing to buy into the "story". Perhaps, one can skip over the questionable details, disregard the unfathomable, and glean what good he/she can from the confusing mire of unlikeliness that is the Bible. It seems to me that a conspicuous number of people do just that. Interpretation is simply left to others... or practiced with little regard for its effects or significance. The argument for understandables becomes less a concern and the benefits of belief simply assert themselves... or appear to. Either many people are expressing fake faith benefits, or they are actually living them. That brings two questions to mind. Someone said, "The devil is in the details" (my apologies to the source). One question is this: Is it okay (God?) to simply ignore the details, discrepancies, and absurdities and believe despite them? Another is this: Can one such as me ask questions and have doubts... while searching earnestly and honestly for spiritual peace and redemption... and then be accepted into the peace of God by virtue of his efforts? I cannot believe that self-delusion and blind acceptance alone will earn me salvation when an honest search for the validity of God, answers or not, is attempted with the purest of intentions.

The answers to these questions will undoubtedly be as elusive as the ones elicited by the other questions I have posed in these writings. Anyone who attempts to answer them for me will likely be biased by their belief stance... and I am sensitive to that. What I seem to be left with, then, is...nothing. No answers, no permission to skip things, no inner peace, and no assurances of any kind that I will be considered for grace... or that grace is even real. It is little wonder, therefore, that I hold small hope for whatever salvation might be possible. The people who tell me salvation is possible have nothing more than this two-thousand-year-old book of supposedly valid wild stories to back up their claims. When I ask about the validity of the content, I am answered with blank stares and incredulous wonder that I would even consider its validity at all. Faith, after all, is by definition blind. In every other endeavor that I can think of, blind perspective is regarded as silly, fruitless, or dangerous. Somehow, the Christian dogma is exempt from this thinking.

July 30, 2013... A Parable

There was a man... we'll call him Ed, who was a good man according to the general standards of morality. His only idiosyncrasy was that he bathed somewhat too infrequently. He had a friend... we'll call him Fred, who was also good, and who, by virtue of his goodness, became an increasingly good friend to Ed. Fred however... for whatever reason, seemed to always have a small electrical charge inside him... which he invariably shared with Ed whenever they met. When Fred approached, Ed got a shock... while at the same time, Fred received the inevitable bouquet exuded by Ed. At first, the shock was nothing more than a source of joking... a minor annoyance that neither man was overly concerned with. Likewise, Ed's vague odor was, for the most part, overlooked. Over time, though, the snap of Fred's shocks made Ed increasingly loathe to be around Fred. As much as he liked Fred, the inevitable shock that Ed knew would come made the thought of spending time with his friend more and more undesirable. Fred, too, began to avoid Ed because of the increasingly offending smell. It got so that both men would only wave from a distance or call on the phone. The distant heartfelt wave, and occasional call, seemed sufficient to maintain their status as friends. Neither man realized, however, that their friendship seemed to be waning. Neither considered how sincere friends might allow such a thing. The friendship waned nonetheless... to the point where it no longer could be considered real anymore.

July 31, 2013... Cool Hand Luke

For a while, I was beginning to miss some of the details I have always thought I knew regarding the story of Jesus. Matthew and Mark didn't seem to elaborate enough... things like..."Father, forgive them; for they know not what they do." ...and, "Father, into thy hands I commend my spirit." (Luke 23:34 & 46) When in Matthew and Mark these things were not mentioned, I began to wonder if they were added for flavor by later elaborators. It was therefore comforting, in a way, to find some of the familiars in Luke.

Another observation pertains to C.S. Lewis' comments about how "historical" the account is presented in Luke. It is, indeed, fairly detailed, corroborative, and compelling in its easily acceptable and believable completeness. If there is anything that gives me pause, it is only that I find it quite unlikely that someone... even an apostle... would follow Jesus around taking down his every word. The words, though, are considered unarguably sacred. I don't mean to belittle the teachings of Jesus... much to the contrary, I am quite moved by the consistently (presented) morality that unceasingly seems to come from Him. I wonder, though, who happened to be taking notes when Joseph and Mary, discovering that they had forgotten their son in Jerusalem (!), went back a day later and found Him in the temple... where He exclaimed, "How is it that ye sought me? Wist ye not that I must be about my Father's business?" At the time, Jesus was 12. My own son is not Jesus, but I cannot remember a single instance where I wrote down anything he ever said...ever. Where do these quotes... especially the early ones... come from?

As I understand it, Luke did not write the Book of Luke. This is apparently not unusual in the Bible, since many of the books were compiled using excerpts from other manuscripts and vocal traditions. Luke, in my understanding, was not an eyewitness to the comings and goings of Christ. He borrowed from Mark's writings, sometimes word-for-word, to put together his version of the story (...as did Matthew). In light of this, it does, however, become more difficult to see validity in the corroborative aspect of repetitive reinforcement. If, for example, I was to exclaim that the earth is indeed flat, I would be wrong. But if several people quoted me as saying it, does that make it true? Repetitive reinforcement only works in support of the claim when the information provided is verified as original thoughts from different perspectives.

I wonder how the Bible might have turned out if the assemblers of it had not been biased in their wish to present the story their way using cherry-picked fragments from other sources... and instead, with a desire to get at the truth, presented every version of the story they could find... citing their sources, and keeping bias and interpretation to a minimum. Much of the story was written during, and around, the time of the events. There were "multitudes" of eyewitnesses. Where are the other eyewitness accounts? Were the apostles the only people considered capable enough to convey the story accurately and honestly? Fruitless speculation, I suppose. In fact, though I have searched, I have been almost completely unable to find alternate stories regarding these events... which points to only a very few other possibilities: 1) ...that there ARE no alternate versions, and 2) ...that those who might have presented one were decisively ignored, suppressed or eliminated.

On the other side of the coin... I found Luke to be interesting and almost fun to read... oh, obviously not the unpleasantness, but the elaborated details provided therein made the book descriptively more engaging than most previous books. It was refreshing to read an account that, indeed, sounded more like history than a fable... however one feels about miracles and such. It was well written.

It strikes me as quite odd that we human beings tend to be passionate about our beliefs, despite the fact that our beliefs have, on countless occasions, been shown to be less than accurate, hardly valid, or completely unverified (or unverifiable). I say this with full awareness that I, too, am included in this sweeping statement. More than once, I have regretted a past stance that was later made weak or entirely false. I have come to believe that a willingness to admit error... or the possibility of error... and the willingness to correct errors, is probably a desirable trait of intelligence. Unfortunately, I have encountered few who can identify with that concept. I, myself, was guilty of that very ignorance (as I call it) years ago... as I have previously admitted. Now that I have had an awakening of sorts... and recognize my own potential to think wrongly, I find that considerably more thought is needed before I can wholeheartedly accept any new idea. I do not seem to be as likely to make rash judgments, take sudden leaps of faith, or even allow impulse buying. Perhaps this is simply a characteristic of aging or maturing... if so, better late than never. It is exasperating, though, that this same tendency to deny our own fallible nature all-too-often gets in the way of our own well-being... and that of others. We, probably, are quite likely our own worst impediment to a satisfactory evolution of the human species.

This observation of mine regarding the potential to be too passionate, probably misguided, or just plain wrong is at the root of my reservations regarding the acceptance of what really does sound like a well-crafted and agenda-based tale of deities, miracles, and blind faith. Have we no other wherewithal than to run with the only story we can stubbornly cram into our notably fallible brains? Are we so narrow-minded that we cannot accept that we cannot imagine more? I, for one, understand that I may not understand. I realize that there is always more to learn. Holding a fast stance on anything as lofty and intangible as the existence of God seems to me to be an exercise in incredible stupidity. Faith is all well and good, but an unwillingness to accept our (God-given?) tendency to be wrong is…well…wrong.

August 1, 2013… A Parable

There was a man by the name of Larry who was the local handyman. He could build or fix or improve just about anything and had been doing so for a very long time. His work was recognized for quality and in heavy demand. He was known for having reasonable prices, honesty and he always showed up when he said he would. One of the admirable traits that Larry had was a willingness to teach what he knew to young helpers. He nurtured his helpers and always had a pleasant smile and an extra tool for them to use. Sometimes his protégés would go on to become handymen themselves, but Larry didn't mind… for they were passing on his legacy… and there was always enough work to go around.

There was another man by the name of Harry who was also a handyman in the neighborhood. His stature as such was largely a result of his own praise for his own work and his own merit. His rates were a bit high, but he was generally available sometime next week… or else he would call. He had a large, new shiny truck with all sorts of tool bins and ladder racks and a CB radio. He always had a wink for the ladies and a polished flask to share with the boys. No one really complained too much about his work… it was fine.

One day, after work, Harry went downtown to get a couple of beers. No one really cared much… he always seemed to be able to hold it alright. As he was going home, he turned the corner by the five and dime… but didn't see Larry stepping off the curb carrying a bag of store goods for old Mrs. Howard. Harry ran over Larry and killed him dead. People were horrified and called Harry a drunken murderer. Harry was devastated and went home and hung himself.

Later, after the funeral, Larry's young helpers began to come forth with stories of how Larry, although as nice as the day is long, had paid them to do things that weren't right... sexual things. One after the other they came forward now that the irreproachable Larry was no longer around. There were many who had been hurt... too many. Harry, it was found, had willed what estate he had to a local charity.

August 2, 2013... Does Matter Matter?

I wonder, sometimes, if I might be better served to purchase, forthwith, a smartphone and learn to look perpetually downward and twiddle my thumbs. As things are, I probably spend much too much time simply thinking... though I am not sure how detrimental it may have been for me. Certainly, I could probably have accomplished considerably more of a tangible nature had I dedicated more of my limited time to physical labor. I hope, however, that accomplishments are not measured exclusively on a tangible scale... otherwise Einstein might be demoted to an obscure accomplisher of nothing.

I was thinking, during my three-mile walk this morning, about my recent, on-going, investigation into the intangible side of existence... and its meaning. Suddenly my thoughts turned completely around and I found myself wondering about the physical side of me... and the universe around me. So much has been bandied about for centuries concerning the origin, significance, and fate of our spiritual existences that we may have missed something on the physical side of things. Not having researched this, I am essentially guessing though.

We (humans) often wonder and argue about our souls and beliefs and why we are here and so forth. This morning I began to wonder why Jupiter is here. Why is Andromeda here? Why is my body here? So much has been thrown about regarding Gods and faith and the like, but is my physical existence of concern... and if so, why? God seems to be concerned with my soul and spirit... if I understand the Bible. If my body is simply a vehicle for my soul, which seems plausible enough, what, exactly is Pluto? What is a rose bush? What is a goat? If souls are God's only concern, why does physical mass exist at all? What is the point for a God to create an incredibly large universe that is so fantastically vast that we cannot even fathom its size... or achieve a visit to hardly any of it? If my soul is of such great value to God, what is the value of the ninth-largest hunk of rock in the Oort belt? If a piece of icy rock in a distant asteroid belt is of no particular concern or value as a creation of God, why then, did He create it?

A couple of hundred years ago, atoms had not been invented yet. Microscopes were not of sufficient quality to detect them. Now we find that protons and neutrons and electrons make up atoms, and quarks and neutrinos and muons and upquarks and antimatter also exist on a subatomic scale. What do these quantum particles have to do with my eternal soul? Do they matter? Why does matter matter? Now scientists have discovered dark matter and dark energy... which combined, it turns out, makes up around ninety-five percent of the universe. If these things were not known for thousands of years, were not a consideration for anything at all, and had no part to play in anything, why do they make up ninety-five percent of the universe? Why are they there at all? How can we possibly be so arrogant as to make up "truths" explaining or defining our intangible existence, our souls, and our worth... that totally disregard nearly everything in the entire makeup of the 13.8-billion-year-old universe? Are we insane?

I don't know how many times I have been advised that the Lord moves in mysterious ways that we humans can never understand. If the universe was created on a God scale... for the mysterious musings of God, for a purpose that doesn't concern us, why should I care if I kill my dog? What would it matter if I acquired a particularly effective poison in massive quantities and dumped it into Lake Michigan? How could a nuclear Armageddon that destroyed our entire planet have anything whatsoever to do with God's plan for my spirit? I apologize to those millions or billions of people who for some incomprehensible reason seem to accept the most ridiculous and unsubstantiated of concepts or stories simply because someone told them to. I'm sorry, but people wrote the Bible... and people are notoriously and historically prone to every conceivable "inequity" as bemoaned by God, Himself... who supposedly created them.

August 9, 2013... Desire & Need

I have mentioned that I have a sincere desire to find some sort of valid path to follow with respect to my intangible existence, spirituality, or immortal soul. It occurred to me today, though, that there might be a very fine line between the desire to find inner peace... and the need for it. If I assume (with apologetic reservations) that inner peace... and the desire for it... is a component of my intangible existence, then there necessarily should be a question of whether it is needed or not. Certainly, we of a somewhat tormented nature can physically exist despite our internal stresses, but we still aspire to a psychological or spiritual comfort level that often eludes us for various reasons... substantiatable or not. I DO desire spiritual peace of some sort. It strikes me that I want this, and yet cannot accurately describe what it is that I want.

A couple of questions, then, come to mind. What is inner peace? ...and why do I desire something I don't understand very well. If I define inner peace to myself as best I can, without looking it up, it seems to be something desirable. Peace is good...whether it is "inner" or otherwise. Therefore I want it. Why do I want it, though, when I am not sure what it is or where it comes from, whether it is attainable, or why it matters? I suppose I could say that the lack of inner peace results in the opposite of inner peace... shall I say...anti-peace? That is... something that seems unpleasant and probably undesirable. The Bible might hint that anti-peace is a product of the Devil's workings. Who in their right mind would desire that? ...despite the fact that no one can scientifically or positively identify what a/the Devil is.

I don't mean to be facetious, but it appears that I want something I can't accurately describe, for reasons I can't accurately describe, and I don't want the opposite of it or the lack of it... which I also can't describe, for reasons I also can't accurately describe. Simple.

But what if the desire for inner peace (or whatever) is not a desire at all... but a need? How does one go about determining what a need is on the intangible side of things? If something turns out, alas, to be a need, then at least a partial explanation of why it is wanted presents itself. I want it because I need it. So the why of the want is satisfied, but the why of the need still eludes us. Why do we need? Do we need because God wants us to need? Did He create us to need? If so, why did He create the impediments to fulfilling our needs? Why would God create a needy people who wants the very thing that He offers us if we will only accept His exist-ence... and rules... and salvation... as valid? The conditional fulfillment of the need makes no sense when both the need and the fulfillment of it are creations of God... who supposedly has the wherewithal to create a people who are considerably less trouble in the first place. Is it a test? Why would God feel the "need" to test us when He certainly has the power to bypass that problematic part of the spiritual process entirely? It appears to me that by testing us, God is actually testing Him-self... since we were created to be exactly what He created us to be. It seems to me that He created the entire scheme... the testees, the tests, the answers to the tests, and the reasons for it all, and the questionable results of the whole process. What sense does all this make to us? Why should we care? If I fail the test, I supposedly don't "see God". If I was created by God to do exactly that... what does the test accomplish? If I was NOT created by God to fail the test... and the results are entirely a consequence of my own doing, then why should I imagine that God plays a significant part in my life? I would determine my own fate, would I not?

August 11, 2013... An Exegesis of John

I learned a new word today: exegesis. It is the critical analysis of a written work...often used with respect to the Bible and other theistic manuscripts. At first, I was somewhat gratified to have added to my vocabulary... such as it is. But as I investigated the meaning and use of the word, I soon realized that practitioners of exegesis appeared to be noticeably biased... at least with regard to the "study" of Biblical books. Invariably, everything I read that purported to be a critical analysis turned out to be little more than biased interpretations, not an impartial analysis... as I expected. Once again, the sources that attempted to explain the Bible... used the Bible to validate the Bible. This simply does not constitute a valid analysis in my eyes... and in fact, is quite disturbing and irritating to me. However, disturbing as it is, this practice (using the Bible to validate the Bible) is almost universally ubiquitous. I admit that personal interpretations are unavoidable with regard to the Bible, but interpreters do not seem to respect the right of others to do exactly the same thing.

There have been a few times during the last few months when, as part of a group discussion, I set forth my own observations regarding what I read in the Bible (Old Testament). Invariably, there was always at least one person in the conversation who became offended that I would "pick at" various passages instead of simply accepting them. I was told (more than once) that if I didn't worry about the details, inconsistencies, contradictions, etc., I would more easily find solace and salvation in it. My immediate response (to the chagrin of the others) was, "Prove it." The usual reply was something on the order of, "Well, it says right here..." In other words, they would point out a passage in the Bible to support what claims were being made about it. These self-proclaimed believers would also point out that although the Bible is a compilation of various manuscripts written by many authors, they (the authors) were "inspired" by God, Himself. "Prove it," I said. "Well, it says here..."

My exegesis of the Bible (Am I not entitled to one, too?) has, to date, been rather disappointing. As a rather poor example of a credentialed thinker, my opinions will, no doubt, be largely ignored by those who simply know better. My skepticism (God-given or not) is just not justified enough, informed enough, or wanted enough by others to be anything more than an unsolicited, misguided attempt to sway the opinions of others... when those others are quite happy to remain unswayed. I will reiterate, though, that I am NOT attempting to sway anyone about anything. I am simply writing down my own thoughts about my own observations regarding the Bible and with my own search for a spiritual path in mind. If I appear misguided, it is because... for much of my life, I was... and to some degree... still am. So is everyone else to some degree. I most assuredly do not want to be misguided, lost, unsaved, ignorant, stupid, or without spiritual solace...anymore. These writings are my personal wanderings through the intangible and unverifiable universe.

Now...about John... There is probably little point in detailing whatever inconsistencies or problematic passages I might have encountered in the Book of John. I think I have found enough problems with the previous three quarters of the Bible to suffice in the way of complaints. One principal issue that sticks with me and constantly pokes me is the one regarding how loving and forgiving God suddenly is in the New Testament. I, for one, can hardly accept that God was, in any way, loving or forgiving in the Old Testament. For at least two thousand years, He was constantly punishing the chosen ones for the very things He created them to do. …and He did not limit His punishments to the perpetrators… He often destroyed entire cities… women, children, goats…whatever. He even killed every living thing on earth once because His own plan for human beings wasn't working out. Now, in the New Testament, we (not just the chosen ones anymore) are expected to forget about the old ways and simply accept that God loves us, He wants us to find grace, He forgives our sins (if we follow His rules), He is suddenly merciful (but not if we make the wrong choice), and, as far as I can ascertain, He still wants us to sexually mutilate our children. If I just ignore these issues and accept what the New Testament says, I will be saved. My spirit will reside with Jesus forever. If the Old Testament doesn't count, why then is it in the Bible? If it DOES count, why am I of such great interest to the Great One all of a sudden… when I was simply a nagging impediment to the repeatedly wayward chosen ones for at least two thousand years?

The Book of John, when considered on an emotional scale, is very compelling and includes many of the famous quotes and parables, and miracles that I grew up with. It is well-written and, I might say, inspired in its rendering of the Christ story. It was supposedly written by the youngest of the apostles around 100 A.D. in his later years… sixty-some years after the crucifixion of Jesus. The sheer emotion and passion displayed therein is understandably likely enough to make believers out of many people. Even I, myself, might find believing somewhat easier had the entire Bible been written as well… questionable details or not. John, if it was indeed him, might very well have convinced me to surrender to Jesus by virtue of his memorable lines and passionate sincerity… had I not had the misfortune to read the preceding Old Testament. It is my considered opinion that the assemblers of the Bible made a serious mistake in the inclusion of it (the Old Testament) as part of the Holy Book. The Holy Book, in my humble opinion, is full of holes.

August 12, 2013... God vs Nature

Years ago, prior to my recent and ongoing awakening, I had a tendency to look at everything that is the universe as a question of God's creation versus the random development and unknown origin of nature. They seemed like opposites somehow... both possible, but both mutually exclusive. I now consider this to probably be unlikely and find them to be a plausible pairing... especially in light of the unknown origin of the universe, or at least the big bang. It is also entirely worth considering that nature, as we know it, IS God. We human beings tend to humanize or anthropomorphize many things. Our pets are probably the best example. Many times people have said to me that their dog or cat thinks it is human and is an equal part of the family. We even refer to boats as "she".

I wonder, sometimes, if God might be an anthropomorphic manifestation of nature. What if, a few thousand years ago, during a thunderstorm, a borderline Neanderthal happened to make a joking comment about the weather: "The old man is snoring again."? It isn't inconceivable that the "kick" his fellows might have gotten could have turned into the eventual personification of a God... whose rumblings and snorings created storms. I must say that I have no problem considering the possibility that our God might not HAVE a human-like personality at all. I see it as entirely possible that God (for lack of a better word) is our anthropomorphic explanation for something that we simply don't know enough about (the origin of the universe). We really don't have to assume a personified entity created everything simply because we don't have any other answers for it. I can just as easily say that it didn't happen that way. Not knowing is not grounds for the justified sanctification of a deity-based idea. We humans are entirely too arrogant, self-righteous, and presumptuous.

August 16, 2013... Acts and Facts

The Book of Acts (of the Apostles), I must say, is probably the most interesting of all the Books I have encountered so far. I don't mean to say that I am swayed by what it says, only that several of the questions I have accumulated over the years...got answered to various degrees. I will admit that although I knew about some of what might be called a connection between the Jews and the Christians, I, unfortunately, did not know how Christians and Jews could believe in the same God... and yet be at odds with each other regarding Him. My oversimplification of it is that God... being somewhat frustrated with His "stiff-necked" chosen ones, suddenly (after a couple of thousand years) decided to include the gentiles (the rest of us) as potential beneficiaries of His grace. So now I realize that the Jews decided to (mostly) ignore the Christness of Jesus... thereby falling back on the teachings of Moses and the subsequent prophets, while biding their time for the real Messiah to come along. They (the Jews) apparently are more than willing to believe in past miracles... and the earlier words of God, but not the (then) present ones. How they separated which wild tales of wonder to believe in and which to ignore eludes me. I should think that a God capable of creating the universe, the Earth, mankind, and all the rest, would also be allowed to change His mind about a few things... such as the gentile issue. As for why He might do that...well...that eludes me, as well. It seems to me that a God shouldn't have a need to change the way He does things... unless He made some Godly mistakes or poor choices... but who am I to question His mysterious ways?

One point worth pondering is the prominence of Paul (Saul) in Acts. As I understand it, Acts was written by the same author as Luke, but I found that the writing style varied in different sections... not that it matters. I suspect that there was more than one author of the Book.

It struck me as a bit odd that Paul, a converted Pharisee who is responsible for the persecution of other Jews, would play such a prominent role in the story of the Disciples... leaving the other original Disciples somewhat in the background. Acts is a lengthy Book... Paul's story is a significant part of it.

The Book of Acts seems primarily to be a record of how Christianity spread after the life, death, and resurrection of Jesus. In this respect, it was quite historical... although mostly from Paul's perspective. I suspect that the perspectives of other Disciples is yet to come in later Books. No doubt, the teachings of the Disciples would have fallen on substantially deaf ears had Jesus not empowered them with the wherewithal (Holy spirit) to perform miracles. This, too, is a question that many others these days, no doubt, ask themselves: "Why was the power to work miracles given so freely to so many in the past, but absolutely no one is blessed with the power now? …at least not in any verifiable way.

I am perplexed a bit about another phenomenon I recently encountered while attending a local church. The Pastor openly preaches that Jesus proclaimed the power to do healing as something any true believer can do while calling upon the grace of God. I will accept my due correction if merited, but I am fairly certain that I remember this gift being bestowed on the Disciples… not just any believer.

Another small thought I had concerns the explicit and complete conversations that are presented by Paul and others. There is no mention of any scribes following Paul around while taking notes of everything that was said in his presence… especially what is described as private dialogs such as the banter between Paul and his Roman guards. I am beginning to feel the need to investigate some of the sources which the Books of the Bible were drawn from. Perhaps there is no simple way to look into it, I don't know at this point, but it is becoming obvious to me that the Bible is a compilation of writings, statements, stories and history that are presented with no citations, no verifiable resources, no proofs of anything, specific and sometimes lengthy word-for-word quotes with no explanation for their accuracy, authorship or verifiability. I am probably inviting considerable trouble into my life stating this, but if I was to write a book like the Bible… making countless wild and unverifiable claims about Gods and miracles and resurrections and such… and then attempt to push it onto unsuspecting readers as absolute truth… and use the same book to substantiate what is in it, I would be so completely ridiculed and persecuted and probably institutionalized, that I would never be heard from again. I defy anyone to tell me otherwise.

Acts is compelling in one significant respect: it details some of the works of the Apostles in very passionate and eloquent language. Paul's (Saul's) wording sounded quite familiar… the very phrases I heard in church these two thousand years later: "Jesus Chris our Lord…" and "…in the name of Jesus Christ" and "…by the grace of God" and "…gave up the ghost." It is really quite amazing that the word-for-word usage of these same phrases has not evolved into somewhat different variations of the original phrases… a common enough phenomenon in the world of languages.

It was also interesting to discover, historically speaking, what the Disciples did when their Holy leader went His way. My own vague recollections were that they (the Apostles) simply continued the work of Jesus in preaching about the grace and salvation of God. Although this is generally what happened, it was interesting to learn about their individual exploits. I was, in truth, a little perplexed at the abrupt ending of the Book of Acts, but I can understand only too well how a man like Paul (Saul) might have been of considerable concern to the Romans. It is not known what became of Paul after landing in Italy, but it can be assumed that the author of Acts simply was unable to continue the story... for various possible reasons. If, for instance, he was killed or imprisoned, that would do it... and he was, after all, sent to Rome to be judged. So...the book ended suddenly.

August 20, 2013... Accountability and Redemption

Today's thoughts are still organizing in my head as I write these words... which is as it should be if my assessment of myself is correct: I think and write much more coherently than I think and speak... having considerably more time to consider my words. Potential readers, then, are spared my stumbling, groping, sometimes futile attempts at vocal eloquence.

This morning's three-mile walk produced a spark that I have been fanning for a couple of hours until this very time. It concerns the ideas of accountability and redemption. It occurs to me that, again, they are not mutually exclusive since I can imagine redemption following accountability, but I wonder about how these concepts apply with regard to me. And then there is the larger issue of how they generally apply to other, perhaps Bible-ized people.

First, I will think about myself. As I stated early on, I am a victim and result of my upbringing... as everyone is. I bear responsibility, however, for the many mistakes, poor choices, and outright sins I have committed... whether explained away or justified by dysfunction or not. I wonder, though, about the difference between how my inequities relate to my physical existence compared to how they relate to my spiritual or intangible existence. Here is a hypothetical example. Suppose I stole from a store window. It is a crime to do so, and I am liable for the physical act of my crime. When I am caught, I am condemned, judged, and incarcerated appropriately. These are physical consequences for my physical acts. I am held accountable and judged accordingly. Once my period of punishment has elapsed, I am considered socially paid in full except for the inevitable lingering social scars. On the spiritual side, things seem a bit less clear. The physical crime is a manifestation of spiritual weakness or misguided reasoning. Some questions arise as to whether these things are intentional thwarts of the law... or the result of unavoidable dysfunction in my personality. Should one be handled differently than the other? Who can reliably determine the difference? Should it matter? Is a crime a crime no matter what? Should mitigating circumstances be considered? ...and then there is this... What if I am sorry for my actions and ask for forgiveness with a promise to learn from my mistakes? Does this matter?

The laws of man are obviously necessary for the continued peaceful workings of society... considering the inherent proliferation of adverse workings. The laws concerning spiritual acts seem necessary for the same reasons... although it becomes less clear about what laws are needed, who has the authority to create them, interpret them, administer them, enforce them or review them for relevance over time. Where is punishment merited and where is forgiveness called for? Do social scars give way to spiritual redemption? Is spiritual redemption possible only after physical accountability? Can someone be forgiven and granted redemption in lieu of punishment? The Bible says (In Romans) that God's spiritual grace supersedes the laws of man. Should an avowed Christian who makes a mistake and commits a crime and is repentant be forgiven and let go... conditionally or otherwise? Where do the "workings" of society end and the "workings" of God begin?

I wonder about the meaning of redemption. Like many words in our English language, it has more than one meaning (in my own words): 1) It is the act of purchasing something by doing something or paying for something. 2) It is forgiveness and grace that was purchased FOR us by Jesus giving His life to pay for our sins. Although I understand these concepts, I wonder how they apply to my discussion of the physical versus spiritual worlds. For instance, if my redemption through Jesus pays for my sins can I expect other believers to acknowledge His payment for my inequities... and consider my debt to society paid? I should think there would be countless prison inmates suddenly finding Jesus with expectations of forgiveness and redemption. If the salvation of the Lord does NOT supersede the obligations to society, then how could anyone find an overriding significance to it? In essence, we would be legislating our way around the Word of God. I think the Pharisees had a problem with that very thing. So if God had a problem with the Pharisees, would He not also have a problem with our legal system... which assigns punishment to criminals despite their avowed status as earnest believers?

I have many questions that will likely never be answered to my satisfaction. It is a nagging wonder to me that with so many justified laws and so many sanctified rules... there is still so much vagueness, uncertainty, biased interpretation, and passionate dedication to questionable or poorly understood ideals. It is disheartening, indeed, to make a concerted attempt to sort out these things... over a considerable amount of time and with a sincere hope for some kind of spiritual direction, only to find a more confusing mess of uncertainties than I started with. The more I learn, the more I am beginning to regret learning. Thomas Gray, who said, "Ignorance is bliss" was likely on to something, I'm afraid.

August 21, 2013... Romans and Omens

If ever there was a written work that adequately describes how Christianity works, Romans is probably that work. Assuming that it was written by a person who personally talked to Jesus after the resurrection, and who took that conversation to heart enough to convert, it details how the entire salvation process works... both for Jews and Gentiles. There were confusions to be sure, such as "...Jews first, and also the Greeks." Supposedly, this is to mean that God will not play favorites anymore... and that anyone supposedly can find salvation through Jesus. This is, as stated earlier, definitely not how God operated for thousands of years. He DID play favorites, however well that worked for Him. Now, though, Paul explains in detail how through Christ we can find our way to God... thereby avoiding eternal damnation on judgment day.

I am a little confused, however, about the fear of God, love of God issue. Whereas for many previous centuries, God's strategy for his chosen ones was to rely on the fear of God to accomplish His goal of "saving" His sinners, His new strategy involves the willing acceptance of Jesus and the love of God... in order that those same chosen one sinners (and now the Gentiles, as well) might find salvation. I wonder, though, about the threat of a judgment day looming in the uncertain future. Are we expected (by God) to lovingly embrace His promise for eternal peace? ...without the fear of retribution which was a component of His work in the past (love of God)? Or are we to embrace the Lord's loving offerings of eternal grace... but only so long as we do it before a certain date (fear of God)?

There are numerous references to the New Testament being based on the love of God. It appears to me, though, that what is called an offering of salvation based on the love of God is followed up with a threat of eternal damnation on judgment day... for anyone who doesn't comply with the "offering". This, I'm afraid, sounds like spiritual blackmail to me, though I will probably need to pursue this issue further after I have finished my unguided tour of the Bible.

As I understand it, an Epistle is a written work in the form of a letter, but for the examination or benefit of anyone. Romans is written to and for the Roman people, Jew and Gentile, and pagan alike. It is meant to be a non-threatening invitation to nonbelievers to become believers... as well as reinforcement to the Christians who already have a Christian faith. Its eloquence is, again, compelling. I feel that I am beginning to understand how a person like me, with all my nagging questions and concerns, might simply leave the frustrating earthly concerns behind and simply accept the admittedly tempting doctrine... right or wrong... in the interest of taking a spiritual break of sorts. I do, after all, supposedly have a choice. I can dwell unendingly on the contentious quirks and interpretations of skepticism, or I can simply dump all my concerns and take on a new set of criteria on which to operate under. Even if I were to become the very gullible believer I fear is a possibility, I might find myself living a more peaceful and hopeful life... however sensible my conversion turned out to be in the end. What, then, is worse; a healthy skepticism that prevents me from finding any real peace for my soul, or a deluded belief in wild tales that can never be substantiated, but that promises everlasting redemption and salvation? I am beginning to consider the possibility that, right or wrong, believing or operating, either way, is essentially the same thing: a personal choice, a leap of faith.

August 22, 2013... Of Ignorance and Stupidity

Some people don't seem to know enough to get in from...out of the rain. They are often thought of as stupid. There is at least one, though, that likes the rain... likes to go out in it... doesn't mind getting a little wet, and finds the whole experience one of unexplainable and irrational comfort and peace...somehow. That one is me. I have always felt that way about the rain... and I don't know why.

This morning, while on my nearly daily three-mile walk, I was forced into an old barn along the road to wait out a warm and steamy early morning storm. I considered, momentarily, that I might be that often referred to stupid person. But as I stood there... comforted as I was by the warm and windy downpour, I realized that stupidity is not actually something I have jurisdiction over. It is a judgment that comes from others... or that is directed toward others. Declaring myself stupid would be an absurdity... a stupid person (I should think) would be too stupid to recognize stupidity. That would be stupid. I, therefore, declared myself unqualified to judge myself stupid... which seemed considerably smarter to me.

But then... I started to think about what stupidity means. As a judgment about... or from... others, it is often facetious in its use... or derogatory by intent. I suspect, though, that it is rarely accurate, and hardly measurable. I also thought about ignorance... stupidity's first cousin... and I decided to clarify, to myself, which is which. Whether accurate or not, I formulated definitions in my own mind... for the benefit of no one in particular. I will say then, for my own account, that stupidity is a state of mind that allows an act despite understanding, while ignorance is a state of mind that allows an act in the absence of understanding.

There will undoubtedly be people who will see these writings as an exercise in stupidity. They might base their judgment upon their own personal definitions of what stupidity is, which of course, is every bit as valid as any judgment I, myself, might make. Is it an accurate assessment of what I do, though? I do not believe I am stupid... or that any of my acts are due to stupidity on my account. I have, however, already professed a degree of ignorance in what I do. I readily accept that I suffer from an absence of understanding regarding my intangible existence, its origin, the realness or form of it, and its fate. These writings are an attempt on my part to minimize the unavoidable ignorance I believe all people operate under. During the last ten years... since the beginnings of my personal awakening, I have tried to recognize, and deal with, my own ignorance. Prior to that...I was apparently too stupid to see how ignorant I was.

August 23, 2013... The Relevance of Faith

I have grown over time, and especially in recent years, to despise hypotheticals. All too often, they are thrown about in conversation to illustrate a point that isn't relevant to the specific issue at hand. Most of us probably don't recognize that we use this unfair and likely irrelevant tactic probably all too often, but we do it nonetheless. But in all honesty, using hypotheticals does have at least one occasional redeeming quality: it invites us to think outside our invariably narrow-sided box...as long as we know enough to distinguish between what is possible and what is really happening.

What if...God is entirely a creation of our limited human imaginations. What if...our souls are really just an interpreted manifestation of electrical pulses whirling around in our brains. What if...where our intangible existence comes from and where it goes... is simply wishful thinking. What if...the passion we exhibit in our beliefs is an evolved behavior that is totally meaningless in the unthinkable vastness and timespan and significance of the universe. What if...what we believe is simply and without question...irrelevant. Is it really so difficult for us to imagine that rampant and ubiquitous randomness might very well exist? What gives us the idea that our ideas have any real significance at all? Why do we want? What if...why(?)...doesn't matter? How can we rationally imagine a Heaven, without any evidence, whatsoever, to substantiate it... and then aspire to go there?

For at least a few years now, I have considered the possibility that we don't have answers to some of our most important questions because our most important questions may not be important at all. Without something more substantial to go on, religious faith is essentially little more than a concept... with nothing more than compellingly-written wild tales (set down by humans) and almost meaninglessly old and outdated historical traditions (told by humans)... to give it validity. It might be entirely possible that we believe because we want to believe... and we don't really even know why. I should qualify, though, that I am not discounting other possibilities in saying these things. It is just as possible that God really does reside...out there somewhere... whether in another dimension or in some sort of undiscovered spiritual place. We have recently discovered the very real, but very invisible existence of dark matter and dark energy. Perhaps someday, we will also discover a dark place... maybe we can call it the dark dimension, or maybe more appropriately the light dimension. Maybe dark energy IS the aggregate sum of all of the consciousnesses or souls who ever lived...or will live.

If we are capable of exercising what we think of as faith, does faith actually exist? If we can say (in writing) that God is both a Father and His own Son at the same time, does that make it true? If I exercise my God-given gift of skepticism in the direction of God, Himself, am I in trouble? ...or am I using what God gave me... in the way He intended... and in fact, doing the right thing? Is it even possible to discredit or offend a creator that might not exist? I do have my questions, don't I?

One other aspect of this discussion concerns the value of faith or a particular way of thinking. Is it better to think one way than another? Is there really any true harm in choosing a way to think at all? Should I simply declare my new status as a Christian believer... and commit myself diligently to it, for no other reason than that there is no harm in doing so? As much as this seems silly to me, it really is no different than NOT believing for the same reason. So what do I have to lose if I tell myself to honestly and earnestly dispose of my inhibiting concerns and take the leap of faith? What is the downside? ...that I will be embarrassed when I die and find myself nowhere (spiritually) at all? ...that other hapless dead people might ridicule me as they pass me by on their way to some very real and (as yet) undiscovered spiritual dimension... for which I do not have a ticket? Could it be that I can choose salvation through Christ and God simply because no one has set forth any other possible scenarios for the continuation or metamorphosis of my intangible existence? Is it possible that it is wiser to consider the lesser of two evils... and choose God simply because NOT choosing God has fewer advantages? I suspect that believers would say, "Go for it. What have you got to lose?" Non-believers would probably say, "Who cares?" Agnostics might say, "Well, I don't know. Maybe you should drive yourself crazy with pointless and endless questions until you die anyway." There is probably something to think about in this.

August 30, 2013... Epistle, Apostle... Let's Call the Whole Thing Off

Although I, admittedly, have more yet to read in the New Testament, it seems a little odd to me that Paul (Saul) plays such a dominant role in the Bible... especially in light of the fact that the real disciples spent considerably more time with Jesus, both before the resurrection and after. They were supposedly privy to much more sacred teachings, miracle works, prophecy, etc. So far, the Books of Matthew, Mark, and Luke were simply general overviews of the entire life of Jesus. The Acts of the Apostles went into more of what happened after the crucifixion, but even a significant portion of Acts is about Paul...who was Saul... the former Pharisee and persecutor of believers in Christ. Paul allegedly had one post-crucifixion encounter with the newly resurrected Jesus... and suddenly, by virtue of his learned eloquence, he is a self-proclaimed and authorized traveling crusader and spokesman for the entire Christian faith. Although this scenario is indeed possible, and not beyond acceptance, it does seem a bit odd to me... almost as if the Bible assemblers recognized Paul's obvious eloquence and passion...and put an emphasis on it to perpetuate their religious agenda. This is, I admit, my nagging skepticism manifesting itself again, but...what harm is there in considering possibilities? I wouldn't entertain... even for a second, the idea that I might influence a believer from believing... especially since I am actively and earnestly looking for something valid to believe in myself.

One issue I have been wringing out lately concerns the various denominations that have evolved over the last two thousand years. If the Book(s) of Corinthians is a mainstay of the New Testament... and it looks to me that it is, then it would seem that the fracturing of the Christian faith into various versions shouldn't happen. Paul plainly preaches the benefits of speaking uniformly and having no divisions among us. Yet, it seems that we (stiff-necked?) sinners persevere in interpreting the gospels in myriad ways, breaking off into separate factions of "true" believers, and declaring our views on the whole thing righteous and indisputable. So much for Paul.

Another point worth mentioning (from my perspective) is in regard to "speaking in tongues". Readers of this manuscript will have to excuse my directness, but...what the Hell is that all about? What can a sudden outburst of some questionable foreign language have to do with anything? ...especially in light of 1-Corinthians:10? Paul plainly states that we all should "...speak the same thing and that there be no divisions among you; but that ye be perfectly joined together in the same mind and in the same judgment." He later explains that speaking in tongues is alright so long as there happens to be an interpreter in the house... but that the emphasis should be on prophesying, not tongues. I don't remember Jesus talking about any of this... and He seems to have had scribes following Him around taking down direct quotes comprising all the pertinent scripture throughout His lifetime. There may come a time when I might accept Jesus as my savior, but I can assure anyone who might stumble upon these words that I will never...never...accept speaking in tongues as anything but rubbish. God supposedly created us in His image... therefore, He obviously has a sense of humor...and, alas, here it is.

Paul also describes how women should behave in a Christian world. He spells out how they should cover their heads when praying... and how men should not. Women should serve men as men serve God... as man was created from God, but woman was created from man (by God). He (Paul) also states that women should have long hair and men should not. Why, then, did God create them both with the same capability and tendency to grow hair to any length? Again, I have no recollection of Jesus ever dictating how hair growth might have anything whatsoever to do with the salvation of our eternal souls. Paul was formerly a Pharisee... known for making up their own rules that went beyond the teachings of Jesus.

Could it be that a measure of Paul's former Pharisee-ish practices might have seeped into his enlightened and subsequently redeemed believer life?

September 1, 2013... Another Letter 2 Corinthians

I must say that I am a bit confused about Paul's (supposedly) second epistle to Corinth. He essentially underlines much of what he preached in 1 Corinthians, but also seems to curiously have a need to justify what he calls boasting. He also appears to be somewhat conciliatory toward those in Corinth that might have had some kind of problem with his status as an Apostle... he was, after all, not one of the original disciples chosen by Jesus. If I have an issue with anything, though, it is perhaps Paul's tendency to drone on about what he sees as his concerns. He lays down carnal and spiritual guidelines that he says are the teachings of Jesus... though his letters obviously interpret what he learned from his brief encounter with Jesus... and the teachings of his "brethren", the disciples. These epistles, for the first time in the Bible, explain and expound on the teachings, but Paul does not explain how he came to understand them so completely. His chat with Jesus certainly could not have resulted in such a broad understanding of the very ideas he was against earlier. One can assume that the disciples filled him in on many points, but where are the comprehensive, detailed explanations from the disciples themselves? Why does the Bible rely on the words of an ex-Pharisee to explain the Gospel when there were perfectly good, long-term, eyewitnesses to everything Jesus did and said? Paul was obviously a gifted writer. Perhaps the disciples deferred to Paul's eloquence and literary abilities simply because he was good at it.

Paul was, no doubt, passionate about his role as Apostle, although I see no rational reason why his suffering should be seen by him as a good thing... scripture or not. Faith is all well and good, but the real world is...well...real. Despite the desire to find spiritual peace and salvation, we lowly humans are still real, struggling in a real world, and working our way through the apparently necessary physical phase of our existence. I for one don't see any reason whatsoever to ignore or justify the very real sufferings we invariably have... and actually celebrate them. While it probably is true that adversity can be seen as an opportunity to make improvements (a good thing), one doesn't have to actually enjoy adversity... as Paul seems to have.

It is disappointing to me that it is Paul who elaborates on the teachings of Jesus... instead of Jesus, Himself. He (Jesus) had many years to make His ideas clear and concise, instead, He chose to use parables and easily-misunderstood abstract language to communicate His lofty ideas to a largely ignorant people. This hardly makes sense... which is born out by two thousand years of factious and often violent interpretations of His teachings. God, Himself, was critically disheartened by the repeatedly stupid behaviors of His chosen people. He even wiped the slate clean and started over once to illustrate it. Now, in the New Testament, He changes His strategy and sends His "Son" to preach love and forgiveness... when for a couple of thousand years He practiced a decidedly cruel and unforgiving regimen of justice based on fear. Then Paul comes along and plays the expert, validates himself, and is somehow accepted and revered as a principal player after having lived a life of chronic persecutions inflicted on the very people he expects to follow his words. Well, I could simply overlook all this and...

September 3, 2013... An Intermission Regarding Anger

It is most frustrating to me that I live with deep-seated anger within me. Born of ignorance and misfortune, it has festered and manifested itself in myriad ways that have been relentlessly nagging and unerringly detrimental to my psychological well-being... and that of others. I am both, aware of it, and abhorrent of it, but seem to be quite unable to deal with it adequately. I fear that I will never find peace... and will at some point die in a muddy mire of quicksand regret, unrelenting emotional torment, and, possibly worst of all, facing an emptiness of spirit deserving of nothing and destined for exactly that.

Should I not be angry when the world has inflicted its inequities onto me? If I blame myself for my own state, does it make the result any less troublesome to me? Is there no spiritual redemption or emotional peace for the likes of me? The proponents of Jesus would say, "Yes". But what do those same people know that I do not? I have read most of the Bible. Many others have not, but somehow are able to reconcile their own failings in Christ. My skepticism regarding the Bible is looked at by others as a detriment to my own best interests... even though my skepticism is God-given and exercised with a vigorous regularity. These others pity me in my torment and denigrate me in my refusal to go quietly into belief as they have. They justify their condescending evaluations as the valid observations and accurate findings of people who have "been there, done that". Who, though, can look in the mirror and see me there staring back?

Although there most certainly are many reasons for anger in people, mine can be characterized as aggravated resentment. I know that I was both ignorant and psychologically compromised in earlier years... a state that resulted in mistakes for which I am both responsible and repentant. My repentance, however, has not resulted in forgiveness or understanding or even acknowledgment. It is difficult to be anything but angry about that. How much in the way of apologies is enough for what one has done? To what degree do earnest changes to rectify failings satisfy those who were hurt by indiscretions? Is there a point at which I can feel my debt has been paid? Jesus says "Yes". He paid my debt. So how does that improve my relationship with those to whom I transgressed? If Christian believers declare their sincere belief and acceptance of Christ and His teachings, why then am I not forgiven by them? Where is the redemption? What is wrong with this picture? Is it reasonable for me to look for redemption from other people instead of Christ? Are these other people not supposedly acting on God's behalf as declared Christians? If I am the cause of an indiscretion to someone, and then I apologize sincerely, try to rectify my wrong, and earnestly attempt to change my ways, is it unreasonable to expect forgiveness and redemption from that person? Does the redemption from God supersede the long-held grudges of normal people? I, personally, do not believe so. People were given the wherewithal to feel contempt and hold grudges and even forgive. How can I ignore these God-given traits? I absolutely DO find the resentment and contempt of others personally disturbing and eminently disheartening. Are my own feelings not also God-given? When do I and my fellow human beings finally chalk the whole thing up to hopeless confusion and simply let it all go? It doesn't appear to be in my immediate future.

September 5, 2013... The Galatians Consecration

As I understand it, Paul's epistles in the bible are not presented in the order they were written. Indeed, after two thousand years, it is difficult to determine the exact dates for the various things that happened. Much of the timeline is based on hints from within the Books themselves... and not on any specific and official documentation or citations. Galatians is thought to be one of Paul's earliest... if not THE earliest epistle written as part of his distance learning campaigns...not that it matters.

Again, he appears concerned that the people to whom he writes have corrupted the meaning and significance of Jesus and His teachings. They apparently have, perhaps unwittingly, confused the righteousness of the law with the righteousness of the Gospels... and have therefore veered off the Christian path somewhat (according to Paul)... and begun a variation of the Gospels that might be described as the first denominations of Christianity. Paul unequivocally denigrates the Galatians and makes a gallant attempt to explain the difference between their laws and the Gospels. My only issue with the whole thing is that, however much Paul seems to want the Gospels to supersede the physical laws, the real world (again) is real. It requires more than spiritual guidance and forgiveness to work effectively. If we human beings are relegated to live through physical existence, then we necessarily must find ways to make our interactions with our fellow humans workable. Our carnal laws do that for us. If I remember correctly, it has been stated in the Bible that we must live a physical life in order to acquire any kind of spirituality. It comes first. It would seem, then, that our earthly laws, too, should come first. But then...my logic is only sensible if others agree with it. I really can't make that claim.

September 6, 2013... A Confusion of Wits

From time to time, I find myself face to face with opposing views regarding one thing or another. Although I have demonstrated a willingness to express strong feelings in this work, I really do attempt to respect the views of others... at least as much as I am able to. Like most people, I occasionally find myself allowing passion to drive a point across... often in an unanticipated and undesirable way. What might be called "wits" substitutes for true sensibilities or considered caring. As much as I know I am guilty of this, I am also sorry for it. There are so many ideas and beliefs that cannot be adequately described in a way that everyone can accept. They are often taken to a tangent that is nearly impossible to reconcile. We, therefore, have disputes and misunderstandings, and even wars.

I sometimes wonder about the rightness or wrongness of our ways... and whether any of it even matters at all in the broader scheme. Somehow, I feel that what I need or want is important enough to struggle for... even though a hundred years from now no one will care in the least. For some reason, I will take a stance on some probably stupid point and dig in my heels to defend my perspective and jockey for position. Then, after a suitable and much too lengthy time, I will simply drop the whole thing as no longer worth the trouble. Looking back, I cannot specify even one instance in any of my own battles of wits that had any lasting or meaningful significance in the entire scheme of things. Is it possible that I simply don't matter? Is it possible that what I think or believe is no more than a static electrical pulse that I somehow assign meaning to... but that actually is completely irrelevant? Are all fights stupid? Are all fighters wasting time that doesn't matter anyway? Why do I feel like things are important when there isn't a shred of proof that they actually are? Are my wits an accident of nature? ...or a God-given tool that when wielded wrongly will frustrate God, Himself? If my wits are from God, then it stands to reason that the results of using them are also from God. God, therefore, has created His own problems... supposedly with full knowledge that He was doing so. I am beginning to think I might be related.

September 9, 2013... Prose and Cons

My understanding of the Book of Ephesians is that it was written by the Apostle Paul while visiting a Roman institution of incarceration, though Paul only briefly mentions his present status as "prisoner" (Ephesians 3:1 & 4:1). Be that as it may, I began to wonder about the preaching of Paul via his epistles. Although I am certainly no anthropologist of antiquity, I think it is fair to say that the people of the Middle East during the time of Christ were largely uneducated... with no formal schooling in the reading arts. This being the case, it seems a bit odd that the obviously well-educated Paul would rely on his written letters to spread the Gospel effectively. I suppose, though... as evidenced by his prison stint, that he may also have been spreading the Word by other means, as well. It is interesting, however, that his letters were addressed to believers of various churches... and that his expectation was that the letters would be read to the parishioners... or at least paraphrased via interpretation. Fourteen Books of the Bible are Paul's Epistles (depending upon which Bible is your pleasure). It is astonishing to me that all these handwritten letters from two thousand years ago were not only kept... apparently in some permanently safe archive, coincidentally by all the different recipients. It is as if they somehow knew the significance of them en masse, and took the steps independently of each other to protect them for posterity. Although I am in no position to dispute this as a possibility, it seems most unlikely. The letters do, however, exhibit similarities in style that, from my perspective, give them credibility as having been written by one person despite having been saved by many.

My modern sensibilities tell me that slavery is decidedly morally wrong. I realize that past proponents of it did not have the benefit of my own biased views regarding it, though. Slavery was, alas, a fact of life in those days. It seems odd, though, that it appears to be condoned... even by the Christians, when the Gospels clearly state that we should treat others as we would like to be treated ourselves. Paul urges his recipients to be nice to their slaves but fails to suggest their freedom as an ultimate nicety. Is there a hint of hypocrisy there?

He also preaches love and respect in marriage relationships... something I have come to recognize as pathetically mispracticed by avowed believers these days. It appears that a measure of hypocrisy has rubbed off on all of us.

One curious and primary point in his letter pertains to salvation through the grace of God. He explains that through faith, and not works, we can find our salvation by way of Jesus Christ. Immediately following this passage, he goes on to say that it will take hard work on our part to accomplish this salvation. So which is it? ...through faith, not works? ...or by hard work? Obviously, he means working hard at faith... but then this might be interpreted as "works" too. I'm being facetious, but then there is some arguable merit to this dichotomy. Throughout the New Testament we are encouraged to do good works, but we are also Gospelled that it is not through "works" that we will find salvation, but through faith. So apparently what we believe is important, and not what we do... as long as we do only good things (like keeping slaves that we are nice to?).

September 11, 2013... Philippians and Colossians

The Books of Philippians and Colossians share many points of the same message. It is essentially the same message that is preached in Paul's other Epistles... that Jesus is God, the "head" of the church, the only true way to salvation, and the perfect example of how to live a moral life in joy. Both Books were written while Paul resided in prison, and although he certainly did not belabor his imprisonment, he did tend to mention it in each letter. It is surprising how little he seemed to be concerned for his own suffering. He was, in fact, joyful and quite positive in his written delivery.

I found nothing of particular concern in the two Books... similar as they were to his other Epistles of the same time period. If anything, the only issue I had was how easy it seemed to be... to make converts to Christianity. God, Himself, had a devil of a time convincing the early Hebrews to be avid believers. It took decades or even centuries of miracles and angels and direct conversations with various prophets, but even then they were stiff-necked. Now (then), all of a sudden, Paul comes along, has one encounter with the newly risen Christ, and dedicates his formerly misled life to the interpretation and dissemination of the Gospels... with joy and determination. ...and his missionary efforts appear to have converts lining up everywhere to be saved. I don't mean to belittle the significance of Jesus' sacrifice on the cross, but in the fairly small timespan of a few decades, Christianity seems to spread like wildfire... and with nothing more than the testimony of a handful of Apostles to fuel it. It is curious that, with the efforts of a few, great numbers of converts organized themselves into a coherent and legitimate religion in a very short time, despite the difficulties God had trying to do the very same thing for centuries. From my perspective, though, God was very direct, but Paul was eloquent. Perhaps the pen really is mightier than the lord…uh…I mean sword.

September 12, 2013… How To Fail In Life

There are myriad ingredients that, when assembled into a spiritual soup, will produce an entrée that is either a singular delicacy, a forgettable toleration, or an outright affront to the senses. Unless the recipe is tried, the result is guesswork; a hopelessly misunderstood list of separates that do nothing for the imagination… much less the palate. …and if the recipe is attempted, there may yet be a number of experiments required to attain the proper subtle balance of flavors that result in a successful dish. In other words, there is usually and invariably a measure of experimental effort required to perfect the goal.

Without going into the gory details (ingredients) of my own life, I can say with surety that I have no intrinsic, natural abilities as a spiritual chef. Whatever attempts I have made in the past to produce a palatable existence have been at best poorly thought out and marginally successful. As previously stated, however, there was a point about ten years ago when I began to pay attention to my failures. I substituted lessons learned for angry excuses and ignorant justifications. But…I am getting ahead of myself.

Although I have given no previous thought to what I am about to write, I will attempt to produce… for the inevitable amusement of those who somehow struggled through my writings to this point… a couple of recipes: 1) a disaster of ingredients suitable for a spiritual dumpster, and 2) a budding delicacy that hints of a hearty spiritual stew, but needs a little work in the way of perfection.

Recipe Number 1: Savory Sewer Soup

¼-ton of finely-honed ignorance… rendered into a sludgy broth
1-heaping armful of emotional and physical abuse… sautéed with vigorously stirred neglect
1 or 2 or 3 whole spankings (beat well)

Add several handfuls of family fights for flavor

A pinch of alcoholism simmered in a fine welfare sauce

Spice with meanness, disrespect, uncare, and poverty

Combine ingredients into a small life and bake on high for fifty years. Add negativity as needed for garnish. Serve daily.

Recipe Number 2: Redemption Stew

1-large tub of life experience... blended on low to a coarse consistency

1-bitter revelation (freshly squeezed)

Several epiphanies of self-realization... grilled to well-done

1-box of possibilities (carefully sorted, peeled, and strained)

1-large forgiveness... preferably home-grown

A generous sprinkling of love and caring for flavor

Combine ingredients into a large fool and shake vigorously until nearly exhausted. Sample results and adjust ingredients to taste. Add acknowledgment for garnish and serve daily.

It is my experience that most people are unfortunate and blatant examples of how not to make people. Many will appear to be better than others in one way or another, but so far, I have yet to find one person who is beyond the need for minor repairs at the very least. I would suggest, as a matter of guesswork, that there are considerably more people in need of professional diagnostics and major repair work than those who don't. What is worse, perhaps, is that the required work will likely be seen as unnecessary, unneeded, or too difficult to be worth paying for... but my experience also tells me that we will invariably pay nonetheless, work or no work.

I mentioned earlier that one of the unexpected side effects of my own revelation ten years ago was that when I discovered my own inequities and failings... slowly but surely, I also saw them in others. My own list of repairs was long enough... and disheartening to behold, but I had absolutely no control over the work needed by others. My long and imposing list of things to do appeared to be almost beyond my ability to contend with, but regardless of what I happened to accomplish on my own, I still felt the inequities of others relentlessly pinching me from all sides. I have believed for some time now that I only have control over about half of what affects me... and the rest is what life throws my way. If what life throws is as compromised as my own throwings were, then I will still have to suffer through a considerable mess of human idiosyncrasies above and beyond what I happen to have control over. My disappointment over my personal failings is supersized due to this.

Failing is easy. All we need do is relinquish our responsibility toward ourselves and allow the uncertainties and undesirables of life to supersede our willingness to contend with them. Some people succumb to failings with characteristically common ease. Others detect the sting of growing adversity on that path and make an effort to find a better one... blindly or not. And somehow, a few are able to cope and adapt and turn adversity into opportunities to change things for the better. I believe I have graduated to the second group... those who realized and admitted their weaknesses and wrongnesses and who attempted a comeback of sorts... to find a more correct direction for their lives. It feels like the right thing to do, but it is, alas, quite difficult and fraught with distractions, frustrations, setbacks, and mortality.

My wife asked me to list my top three needs that, if satisfied, would help me to be happy (read: content...in my view). They are in no particular order: acknowledgment, redemption, and love. Acknowledgment means that I need to be seen as I am... not as "someone who...". I need to be accepted as more good than bad and valued as a valid, worthwhile, and desirable human being. ...easier said than done. Redemption means that whatever I might have unwittingly or inadvertently done previously in my life that adversely affected others or myself... might be forgiven...and not just by God. Love...well...no one can adequately describe what this means, though everyone seems to know that they need it, what it is like when they receive it, and its value. I don't just want it; I need it... same as everyone else.

I am hardly the qualified expert to consult when attempting success in life, but as far as failing in life is concerned, I think I may be able to be of some assistance. I have, after all, little of value to offer as valid and worthwhile advice based on successful strategies. My own life has predominately been a dismal disappointment... with only the last ten years of difficult struggling to account for whatever positive changes I might have achieved. If I was to offer my best advice on how to make a life...good, it would be to NOT listen to me and find someone who is actually happy (or content) to drag you along with them. I am not there yet... although I am working on it and, perhaps, making progress.

Peale's book on positive thinking contains intriguing ideas on how one might attain a measure of contentment and peace in an otherwise lacking life. Though there is Christian dogma entangled with the advice, its critically gleaned information seems to be worth some effort to try. In fact, any effort to rectify behaviors that don't work well is preferable to no effort and continued suffering. My journaling journey through the Bible is also just such an effort... hopefully one that results in something better for my intangible existence. I have to think that even the consideration of alternative ideas will be of some benefit... even if I don't eventually find an acceptable and generally beneficial path. I find it difficult to believe that ignorance and blind acceptance is the only way to make faith workable. I may be wrong about that, but I hope I am not.

September 16, 2013... A One and A Two...

1 & 2 Thessalonians are interesting departures from Paul's other letters in that they dwell less on Paul's qualifications as an Apostle... and the preachings resultant from that status... and more on what is often called the second coming of Christ. Avid interpreters of the Bible will find myriad points of confirmation, no doubt, that the second coming is foretold, inevitable and clearly explained. I, personally, did not find much more than brief, vague hints regarding it... previous to Thessalonians. In fact, the very reason I have not addressed this topic prior to this paragraph is precisely that I simply did not see it presented in the Bible in any conspicuously clear and noticeable way before Thessalonians. With the addition of orchestrated interpretation, any topic can be declared obvious and significant, but I

simply did not see it. I will, however, defer to more knowledgeable and observant readers of the Bible...than I.

Paul makes several statements regarding judgment day, salvation, Satan, and Jesus... that are...well...the Gospel, despite the fact that none of these statements were substantiated by any previously elaborated passages. Oh, there were brief mentions here and vague parables there, but I should think that something as significant as judgment day and the salvation of our souls would be explained in no uncertain terms, plainly and unarguably, by Christ, Himself... considering that He came to see us for that very reason... in person. Instead, we are graced with confusing new ideas that are neither spelled out clearly nor left as uncompromisingly undeniable facts. He does not say, "Do this or you will die like this bad fellow here." He does not say, "Instead of just spelling out what is going to happen, I will have someone send you a letter." According to Paul, the all-forgiving God will accept repentance and conversion only up to a certain date... then you die badly. For thousands of years, we human beings have demonstrated repeatedly... to the chagrin of God, Himself, that we simply do not have the God-given wherewithal to understand, accept or manifest anything in the way of good, consistent, and correct spiritual behavior for any appreciable length of time. It is almost as if we were... stiff-necked.

So now we are warned in a letter by proxy that Satan will appear claiming to be something that he is not (or is he?) and try to lead us all astray for some reason that we are not privy to. Why would Satan care in the least what happens to us. If he has the power to exist as a God (or whatever), influence us to disaster, thwart the all-powerful Lord of the universe, and doom us to everlasting suffering (despite God's best efforts), we might consider wondering why? ...when as an entity that supposedly can challenge God, Himself (according to the Bible...so it must be true), Satan does, indeed, seem God-like to me. God, Himself, said we should not put other Gods before Him... which indicates to me that there are other Gods.

So either Satan exists... and as a god... or he doesn't. If God has the power to collect and administer to my (supposedly) eternal soul... and so does Satan... well... what does that make Satan? If God(s) has the power to create and destroy entire universes... and everything in them, how can we possibly be arrogant enough to believe that the whole thing... the thirteen-point-eight-billion-year-old universe of hundreds of billions of galaxies... each with hundreds of billions of stars... all happens to exist for us? ...and the proof is that Paul wrote us a letter?

This is all very lofty stuff. I find myself feeling quite overwhelmed simply throwing these ideas around. I do wonder how much of my own logic and understanding might just be wrong. No doubt, there are many, many people who would happily dismiss most of my ramblings as the irrelevant and detrimental work of the Devil. I would counter, though, that the Devil... if he exists at all... has no power over me whatsoever if, with nothing more than my own convictions, I can deter his best efforts. Profound, but true... according to the Bible.

September 19, 2013... Tim and Tim Again

It is an apparent fact that much of the New Testament was written by letters from Paul, who allegedly encountered Jesus once... and therefore must certainly have relied on the interpretations and teachings of the other Apostles for what he knew and taught. In the Timothys, there seems to be a considerable amount of detailed guidelines for the continuing day-to-day workings of the church... and those who administer it. Although Paul, himself, proves that letters could be sent and received... despite his imprisonment, it seems odd to me that Paul seems to have all the answers... even though he is imprisoned in Rome for many years... and away from his contemporaries. How can it be that the very Apostles that taught Paul what he knew... and who were free men teaching the Gospel, did not spread this information around themselves? How is it that a few letters from a prisoner in a distant land were so instrumental in the formation, guidance, and maintenance of the new church? I have to wonder if the creators of the Bible... with their specific agendas... might have cherry-picked which "books" of the Bible were pertinent to their obviously orchestrated efforts. I cannot imagine that a group of unbiased scholars could have agreed about anything, much less which books were true enough or significant enough to publish for the salvation of the countless millions who would follow. Am I to put my terribly confused and skeptical faith in a book that was written in no small part by a prison inmate whose only notable credential is the self-declared, one-time encounter with a dead man-God? It is a lot for me to accept.

As for the details... Since interpretation is not my strong suit, I do not feel qualified to make any substantially significant points regarding what is found in Timothy 1&2. I will, however, stumble through a couple of things I wonder about. In 1 Timothy, Paul writes about how God wants everyone to be saved (1 Timothy 1:15). Yet God does not simply save everyone, He tests them... apparently to weed out the ones who should not be saved... even though He wants to save everyone. I see this meaning that we lowly, stiff-necked people have the wherewithal, power, or stupidity to thwart what God wants. He knowingly created us to be capable of thwarting His wishes... and then tests us to see if we will do it... and punishes those of us who fail the test by slamming the door of Heaven in our faces and leaving us to the mercy of Satan... who He must have also created to be what he is and do what he does. It is sort of like setting up a fixed race, with contrived obstacles, against others who don't have a chance of winning... and then penalizing the losers for losing. Is God having fun with this?

There is also the issue of women's submission to men. I realize that two thousand years after the wondrous events of Christ, I cannot be expected to have the same perspective on women's rights as the people of the time did. It is no secret, though, that it was a man's world for the most part. I do not remember any instance of Jesus declaring that women must be subservient to men in any way. Paul, however, preaches this very thing... with the full expectation that his fellow preachers will likewise spread...the Gospel.

Paul briefly describes "the last days" (2 Timothy 3:1) as a time when men will live in sin and act contrary to the teachings of the church. He declares that judgment will be passed at that time by Jesus, Himself, who will relegate those who have sinned to Hell and Satan... while those who have properly suffered and remained faithful to God's laws will be gathered for salvation and live eternal lives in Heaven. Previously, though, he teaches that it is not what we DO that delivers us to judgment, but whether we accept Jesus as God and savior. Paul, himself, is a prime example of this very thing. He was a Pharisee and a self-avowed persecutor (1 Timothy 1:13) who, having repented his sins and having accepted Christ, was forgiven... whereupon he began his new job as Apostle. How then will other sinners be judged by their actions?

Paul also makes reference to how God has stood by him during his period of torment and imprisonment. This, no doubt, is why he was able to send and receive mail.

October 4, 2013... Wrestling With Myself

As I near the end of my self-imposed Bible reading exercise, I am beginning to realize that my personal struggle with my own ignorance, my search for spiritual enlightenment in the Bible, and my admitted status as an agnostic will probably necessitate further exploration of the Christian doctrines... beyond what I have found in the Bible. I am disheartened, this far along in my quest, that the answers I had hoped to find still elude me. The great and powerful Oz, I mean...God, just seems too much like a myth to accept on the basis of a two-thousand-year-old record of stupidly questionable stories that simply should not be so difficult for a God to make clear. God himself has repeatedly shown regret that His own "stiff-necked" people just don't seem to be able to get their act together. How, then, can we be expected to unerringly assemble the perfect and unarguable gospel of God into one great work... accessible to all, and presented as a clear and concise handbook for living? So far, the only lofty lesson I have learned is how incredibly unreliable and universally ignorant and arrogant we human beings are. I, for one, am ashamed, in the face of a potentially real God... that I am part of this dismal mess of humanity. As serious and sincere as my intentional search for spirituality is, I am finding myself incapable of relinquishing my supposedly God-given skepticism in favor of the (also God-given?) peaceful surrender of my soul to Jesus...so far. It is also quite difficult for me to admit this as I am so very ready to do exactly that upon finding valid reasons to do so.

I fully expected that I would find something in the New Testament that would make all the difference in my thinking. Others might say that I am simply not "letting go". I say that I am actively looking for some sort of spiritual guidance that is based on something I can understand and accept as the person I am. If I am failing God's test, then it is because God designed me to fail. He designed a test that many cannot pass... and I appear to be one of those many. He designed Satan and Hell (If they even exist at all)... and if I am relegated to reside there, it is because He arranged for it... otherwise, there would be no reason for it to exist. I am who I am because God supposedly created everyone and everything...even the failures... and the penalties for failing, and the anguish we experience wrestling with it all. Believers will say that I can simply accept Jesus as my savior and all will be well. I say that if I have the power through my own decision-making to convince God that I am worthy of acceptance... or Satan for that matter, then my power must necessarily be on a par with God's. Blasphemy? Prove it. God could have simply made me Godly... He didn't. God could have explained what He is doing with this universe of ours... He didn't. God could have written the Bible Himself... so that we stupid people could understand it as He wants us to... He didn't. This whole thing is flawed through and through. I find it absolutely incredible that millions or billions of people are swallowing it whole. Am I right about this? Maybe not. I don't pretend to have an insight that billions of others somehow missed. I, rather, hope I AM missing something and will find it. For this reason, I expect that upon finishing the Bible I will, in some way, continue looking elsewhere. If I have missed something, I wholeheartedly want to find it. If I have not, then God must certainly have intended it this way.

October 8, 2013... I Am Lying

One of my favorite original Star Trek episodes concerned a "computerized" entity which always seemed to be one step ahead of our heroes... and who appeared to be on an unwavering mission to eliminate anything it didn't understand. Attempts to reason with this entity continuously failed and it was only when Captain Kirk realized that the only way to defeat it was to make it compute itself to death... so he simply said, "I am lying." The entity was immediately and irrevocably confused. If Kirk was lying, how then could his statement be true, and if it wasn't true, how could he state truthfully that he wasn't truthful? The entity short-circuited and the Enterprise flew off into the proverbial sunset.

Although I really have no major issues with the Book of Titus (which I had never heard of prior to this reading), I thought it worth mentioning that this Star Trek-ish dichotomy also appears in Titus (Titus 1:12). Paul states in his letter to Titus that, "One of themselves...said, The Cretians are always liars..."... and in 1:13, "This witness is true." Well...if a Cretian says that all Cretians are liars, how can we be expected to accept the truth of the lie?

Why do I bring this quirky subject up at all? ...because this Book of the Bible is Gospel. Literally. Paul literally states that when a Cretian claims that all Cretians are liars...it is true. What, exactly, is a critical thinker supposed to do with that? ...overlook it? I think not. Are these not the inspired words of God, Himself? Perhaps, with a bit of luck and faith, we might discover that God is not a Cretian.

October 12, 2013... A Questionable Exegesis

After a quick look at Philemon, I had nearly decided to defer comments for some more substantial Book yet to come in the New Testament. Then I began to wonder exactly why this short and flowery Book was included in the Bible, to begin with. As far as I can discern, it appears to be primarily an attempt by Paul to convince Philemon to accept, with open and forgiving arms, the return of Onesimas... who apparently had some previous dealings with Philemon. I did not find it clear, exactly, who Onesimas was or what his business was with Philemon, but it was stated clearly that whatever debt was owed...Paul wanted it forgiven or charged to his own "account". The idea, as I understand it, is that because of the new Christian doctrines, forgiveness and acceptance were expected to be demonstrations of earnest adherence to Christ and His teachings. Paul, through a bit of flattery, seemed to be softening Philemon up in an effort to save Onesimas from whatever fate he would otherwise have suffered at the hand of Philemon. As usual...it's who you know.

October 15, 2013... Misunderstanding All I See

My wife asked me this morning... if we could try to create our own happiness today. At first glance, this seems not only reasonable but desirable... an admirable attempt at…a good day. I'm sure she had only the best intentions in suggesting this course of action.

She would, no doubt, find inevitable faults in how I will have directed my day to unfold, though. For some time now, I have fostered a belief that how we fare in life is an eventual result of NOT ONLY what we, ourselves, do, but also of what happens TO us. Some would argue that it is our reaction to what happens that determines our ultimate state of mind. I do not agree. Despite my best efforts, I would find it difficult, indeed, to convince myself that I could feel peace and contentment… for any other reason… while someone was burning me to death. To be sure, there are stories of just that sort of thing: Joan of Arc, for instance, comes to mind. I have no doubts, however, that, inspiring stories notwithstanding, she likely screamed bloody murder as it happened. I certainly would have.

Perhaps I am simply not strong enough in spirit to block my own negativity with a concerted and successful program of positivity with which to overwhelm any unpleasantness I might otherwise experience. This is probably true. I do not claim to be spiritually blessed in any way. This is the primary reason I am attempting to find a valid direction for my intangible existence to follow in the first place. At this point in my searchings, I am still quite convinced that my environment does indeed affect how I experience my days. I do not believe that I am entirely and exclusively the master of my happiness. I am also concerned, in no small way, that I am not subject to unfounded delusions of self-power. Self-control is, to some degree, certainly valid in my opinion, but it is not the only ingredient in my soup du jour. If someone puts onions in my soup, I will simply not like it… no matter how much I put my faith in some lofty ideal.

So…after all this, I now ask myself if I might be wrong about it. Is it possible that I do not understand how faith works? Is it possible that I really can be happy about onion soup? My wife would probably say that if I was starving and there was nothing else to eat, I would most certainly get to a point where onion soup would seem most delicious. She might very well be right. But I am not starving and I do not like onion soup…and I do not see any reason why I SHOULD like it as things are. Am I, therefore, supposed to behave as if I WAS starving? …or should I operate under my perceived circumstances? …or someone else's?

When it comes to faith, I cannot help but think that the best way to live is the one that is determined by what I am most comfortable with... however right or wrong it might appear to others. It may seem unworkable to others in one respect: that if everyone followed their own "comfortable" path, we would likely have a culture of selfishness and total chaos. I wonder, though, if total chaos is any worse than the organized group chaos we seem to have anyway. So far, my investigations into faith and spirituality have yielded me little more than a nagging and ubiquitous confusion of unsubstantiated stories and beliefs, curious overlookings of Biblical inconsistencies, and many questions regarding the validity of spirituality that are probably impossible to resolve. I do still have some hope, though... a curious enough thing in itself.

If I step back a couple of paces and try to look at the whole spiritual picture... everything as a whole as I see it, I am filled with wonder that such a significant part of who we all are is so apparently and entirely mysterious. I do not see any answers; I see guesswork. I do not see valid and palatable explanations; I see myths and impossibly incredulous hopeful imaginings. I am aware that these comments qualify me for exclusion from accepted... though unsubstantiated... spiritual opportunities. "Believers" will likely just write me off as not worth bothering with. Maybe they are right, but maybe what is right doesn't matter. Maybe there IS no right. Although I am quick to question or discredit much that I have encountered in the Bible, I can find no better explanations for what is going on...in my own bag of tricks. If I am truly honest with myself, I really cannot find the idiosyncrasies or faults of others any less troublesome than my own. I do admit my shortcomings, though... whatever they may be. Far too few will admit their own faults... or even a possibility of them.

October 17, 2013... The Absence of Knowing

Undoubtedly, one of the all-time most curious issues concerning humanity has to be, "Why are we?" I find it most incredible that we humans have come so far in understanding the universe and its quirky workings, yet we really have no hard evidence regarding the what and why of our intangible existences at all. Why is that? No doubt, speculators of a spiritual persuasion will postulate that our souls are not within our area of jurisdiction. I have heard it stated that we do not need to know "why" we are... and that it will become clear when we have shed this physical existence and entered the realm of God. Great. So if the reasons for the mystery of our spiritual existence is denied us during our tangible stay on this earth, how can we be expected to understand the significance of choosing a spiritual path on the basis of nothing more than wild tales and passionate ravings of "experts" who have no more evidence for anything than I do?

I know that I do not know many things. I have come to understand that I do not know these things because I have not learned them. Simply not having learned them, however, does not automatically mean they aren't there to learn. As an agnostic, I have resigned myself to accept that possibilities are viable until they are proven unworkable. I, therefore, accept that God may very well exist... whether in another dimension or in some invisible corner of the observable universe (remember dark energy?). I cannot discount the possible existence of a deity simply on the assumption that if I do not have proof, then there isn't proof. There may very well be proof that hasn't come my way as yet. I do not accept (for no particularly discernible reason) that I have to die to get some answers. If I am wrong about that, fine, but there simply isn't any compelling evidence to substantiate it in my eyes. I reserve the right to question or reject things that cannot be explained by the only senses I was graced with when born as a human being. This right, too, was given me (supposedly) by God... was it not?

October 23, 2013... Perplexing Hebrews

The Book of Hebrews is probably a very good example of what I mentioned a few paragraphs ago... namely the pervasive lack of clarity that I found not only curious but frustrating during my Bible experience so far. Once again, I am intrigued by the presence of a "Book" that does not explain itself. It isn't clear who wrote it, specifically for whom it was written (besides Hebrews, in general), or for what purpose. It, instead, contains an exhortational sermon of sorts that seems to have as its purpose the prevention of Christian adherents from an apostasy back to Judaism or some other prior beliefs... although I am really not very certain of that either.

I found the comparisons between Jesus and the angels singularly odd. I have to think that the author was attempting to persuade the recipients of the "letter" to try and see the difference between the messengers and their boss who sent them. ...in other words, the difference between the Old Testament... with its inspired Word of God expressed by prophets and angels, and the New Testament... with its message preached by Jesus... who is NOT an emissary of God, but God Himself...sort of. But then there is the question of the Disciples and Apostles... who were also emissaries of God, but in the New Testament. Confusing.

So the letter's recipients were encouraged to find the strength and commitment to continue following their Christian belief and not succumb to the pressures and persecutions of nonbelievers... or misguided believers (the Hebrews). They were, likewise, to remember that Jesus made a new covenant with everyone... including gentiles... that supersedes the old one meant only for the Jews. There is small mention, however, that God gave up on His unsuccessful prior plan for humanity and was obliged, by virtue of His own failure, to try something else. Two thirds of the Bible, then... the part regarding the old covenant... is to be considered void, although it is apparently and perplexingly permissible to selectively reference certain passages regularly to press a point.

October 24, 2013... The Father, the Son, and the Wholly Spiritual Connection

The Holy Trinity has been a matter of some intrigue to me of late. Though I hardly qualify, in any worthwhile way, to exercise authority on the subject, I do have to acknowledge my (God given?) ability to wonder about it. I am a father; I have a son, and both of us can sense an undeniable and intangible connection with one another. This alone, I should think, qualifies me in some vague way to investigate the Trinity from my personal, admittedly ignorant, perspective. As I have mentioned before, none of what follows has been preplanned or outlined in advance. I can only hope I do not embarrass myself (or others) by my tendency to think as I write... whether in a worthwhile way or not.

The idea of God the father sort of has a ring to it. For the moment, I will assume that, at least as far as the Trinity is concerned, God is indeed…a father… and not just figuratively as a father of everyone and everything, but as…Jesus' Dad. One would have to assume that when Mary experienced her enviable immaculate conception, that the perpetrator of it was God… after all, He claimed (by proxy) that He had given His only begotten Son. He also proclaimed that He was very pleased with Jesus… and so was, by default, a proud father.

Jesus, being the alleged established Son of God, often referred to His Father throughout His lifetime, but it has been my, perhaps incorrect, understanding that Jesus IS God… but in human form. The Holy Spirit…well…I really don't know what that might be. I will simply call it, for lack of a better description, an idea. One of the principal observations of my critical self-analysis is that I do, indeed, possess an intangible existence of some mysterious sort. I, therefore, have to allow that Jesus had one as well… by default since He was Human. I have not discovered any compelling or substantiated evidence for exactly what that intangible existence actually is, however. Whatever explanations I stumble upon seem to be nothing more than the heartfelt imaginings of various inspired and righteous-minded people bent on making more out of life than what is evident by virtue of our senses. We humans tend to be quite adamant that what we think we understand supersedes what is understood by others… or what is not understood. It should also be understood that understanding does not mean knowing. There is most assuredly a difference… one that is all too often…well…misunderstood.

For the sake of conversation (with myself), I will assume, for the time being, that God is the "Big Guy" in all this, Jesus is some sort of piece of God manifested in human form… His son, and the Holy Spirit is the intangible existence of whatever ties them together. Now, what should I do with this information? Faith appears to be the glue that others use to connect themselves to God. Glue apparently does not stick to God anymore though… since the New Testament. One must go through Jesus to get to God. It wasn't always that way, but now it is… since God changed his mind. So if I somehow DECIDE to have faith (the glue) in Jesus, Jesus will put in a good word for me with God and I will be "saved" from eternal damnation, whatever that is. This agreement, of sorts, by virtue of the Holy Spirit (the connection with God), is binding and irreversible... unless that is, I do not accept Jesus as my Holy Proxy by a certain, but unknown, date... and pending "good works" and adherence to God's law. The Devil will also be thrown in to tempt me for good measure... for whatever reason that I cannot fathom for the life of me. All I have to do to thwart his efforts is DECIDE to have faith... which gives me considerable power over him... and which I would promptly do in the unfortunate circumstance of an encounter with him. If, however, I do not have an encounter with Satan, obvious or otherwise, I am expected to believe in him anyway... by virtue of the negativity that is ubiquitous in the world... and resist him accordingly. What fun.

Humor aside, I must admit that I do not know, in any kind of sensible and substantiated way, what God is. And since Jesus was supposedly created from the same stuff, I also do not know what Jesus is/was. The Holy Spirit is, likewise, an idea that has, coincidentally, no evident verifiable basis in reality. Satan, I'm sorry to say, seems just silly.

I am my son's father. There is verifiable DNA evidence to substantiate it. My son is a "piece" of me... again verifiable with DNA. There is an intangible bond between us that is admittedly elusive. I don't know what it is... and if I never find out what it is, at least I have faith that it is there... and that kind of unsupported belief, after all, is what I am supposed to be trying to achieve in my pitiful life if I am not mistaken. I still hope to find some sort of digestible validity in the Christian doctrine on which I can base my decidable faith, but I have not seen it yet. I will need more than curious questionable stories and interpreted ancient scrolls and well-meant fiery oratories and delusions of grandeur to find the spiritual peace I yearn for. I am waiting. I am open to reasonable and palatable possibilities. Barrage me with stupidity, though, and I will promptly go make a very large dose of popcorn...and eat it with abandon.

Oh, I nearly forgot... I probably should think a bit more about this idea I mentioned earlier that the Holy Spirit might simply be an idea. It occurs to me that many of the worthwhile discoveries of the past began with someone's idea. Some ideas turned out to be dead ends or stupid fancy, but others became the basis for scientific study with tangible results... and even historical and profound truths.

I have neither the requisite training nor the prior credential to attempt any sane kind of explanations for the questions I have wrestled with here, but that doesn't disallow me from discussing my ideas... whether they are palatable to others or not. The very idea of ideas can be threatening to someone who reserves the right to proclaim their own ideas as righteous, but I have to think that one idea is no more valid than another... however preposterous it might be... until it acquires some sort of acceptable basis in reality, scientific or not. Unfortunately, we humans have a considerable history of bad ideas and misdirected loyalties, and loathsome consequences. With that in mind, I prefer to look at questionable ideas as simply that...questionable. I don't mean this in a negative way. Questionable does not mean bad, it means (from my point of view)...needing more study and understanding. That is why I do not consider myself an atheist. God (to me) needs more study and understanding for acceptance to happen. This rather convoluted and drawn-out discussion with myself... in journal form, constitutes that study.

November 3, 2013... Arrogance and Ignorance

Most people will likely agree that a degree of ignorance happens in one form or another, and to varying degrees of magnitude, to just about everyone. If one is able to recognize that ignorance is not necessarily a negative thing, but simply a lack of knowing, then coping with it, or rectifying its influence, is considerably easier. I have noticed, however, that ignorance is sometimes (often?) accompanied by arrogance. That is, people who manifest their ignorance to others are often not only oblivious as to exactly how lacking in knowledge they really are but are also sometimes overly self-righteous in their interactions... despite their sometimes misdirected or unfounded convictions. I discussed the ignorance of being ignorant earlier, but it occurred to me this morning that our arrogance can often go hand-in-hand with it. We can mistreat others by asserting our weak knowledge. We can lose friends by being a know-it-all who doesn't. I have been guilty of this in the past... but as of my awakening of sorts, ten years ago, I have tried to make a concerted effort to be mindful of my own ignorance... its myriad manifestations, and its effects on others.

This mindfulness regarding personal ignorance is probably one of the most important revelations I experienced since I began to investigate myself. The realization that I have been wrong about many things... and that I am probably still wrong about things... and that I will undoubtedly be wrong in the future, has forced me to be more cognizant of how I think and relate to others. I know that I don't know everything and I, therefore, try to avoid condescension, arrogance, self-righteous assertion, and stubbornness. I only wish it could be this way with everyone. As I said before, since I began seeing these idiosyncrasies in myself, it has become glaringly obvious that everyone else has them too... and it is quite disheartening to spend so much time working on my own failings... only to repeatedly run up against the failings of others... especially when those other people are oblivious to their inequities... and are self-righteous and arrogant, too.

Ignorance, by itself, can be excused in most cases because people cannot be blamed for not knowing something. It is only when they refuse to learn... or when they think they know and are adamant (arrogant) in their justifications that they become irritants to others. An acquaintance of mine... who I consider a friend, has been known to say, "I refuse to suffer fools". Although there are certainly times when I have thought that way toward others, I have come to realize that often enough it isn't easy to determine who exactly is the fool. Fools, I have learned, are everywhere. They are us.

Arrogance, then, is an attitude. Attitude, in my opinion, is a learned inequity. What can be learned can be unlearned with some effort and an open mind. Acquiring an open mind is, in my opinion, the process of recognizing and rectifying ignorance in ourselves. It is easier said than done, but better done than not.

November 4, 2013... Understanding James

I will admit, with a certain embarrassment, that I struggled with the Book of James. It seems straightforward enough... with its fairly clearly-stated rules to live by, but there was something in the background of James that just kept nagging me with a troublesome feeling. I read the Book at least two times...and listened to it via CD at least three times... and still felt that I was missing something. Something in there just didn't seem right to me.

Usually, when this uneasiness assaults me, I write. I realized long ago that I was not blessed with a quick mind. If I simply attempt to think out a problem, I will usually end up playing some naggingly catchy song over and over in my head instead. This morning, on my almost daily walk, I suffered through unending replays of Stairway to Heaven. Read into it what you will.

Although I have tried not to make the authorship of individual Books of the Bible much of an issue, this one seems to suffer from a lack of credential. As I have been able to understand it, James was written by one of four James... though it is generally accepted that it was written by Jesus' brother James. Though that alone would seem credential enough for anyone, I am having a little trouble with Jesus' siblings. I realize that people were encouraged to have children during those times... and Mary and Joseph likely tried to do their part, but if Jesus was the son of God... born of immaculate conception... and from a virgin, then Jesus was undoubtedly Mary's firstborn at the very least. If Mary and Joseph begat more children, Jesus would have to be considered half-brother to his siblings, I would think. There are enough references in the Bible to suggest that Jesus' brother James was one of the Apostles (Saint James the Just)... and therefore a likely candidate for author of the Epistle of James.

James preached in his letter that facing trials in life develops perseverance. I'm not sure that was the best choice of words, but it is probably true to some extent. A more commonly known saying is, "Adversity breeds character." James, however, seemed to suggest that people might actively welcome adversity in the interest of garnering some sort of favor from God. I can wholeheartedly understand the significance of the favor of God, but I am not completely stupid... and if I am even remotely representative of an average human being, I can confidently say that I would not sensibly embrace adversity... God or no God. I don't think anyone else would either. For James to suggest otherwise is...well...unrealistic.

God does not tempt anyone. This idea of James sort of struck me as very interesting. I began to think about how God has operated in the past according to the Bible... and sure enough, I don't remember any instances of temptation by God.

He does, however, use trickery (Abraham & son), threats (just about everyone), extortion (believe by Judgment Day, or else…), annihilation (Noah)…and on and on. Satan, however, relies heavily on temptation to sway people away from the (eh hem) merciful arms of the Lord. I am not advocating that people follow Satan, but one has to admit, he does seem to use more humane tactics… however loathsome the (possible) end result.

James also preaches something I DO agree with…that people should be quick to listen and slow to speak. It is only too common for people to serve up a fine meal of undercooked ideas. We actually DO leap before we look sometimes. The old carnival shady would proclaim that the hand is quicker than the eye, but I have noticed that the tongue is often quicker than both. This probably explains why I tend to think better on paper than in conversation.

I am fairly sure that it was Paul who declared that it is only through faith in God and the acceptance of Jesus as our savior that we can find salvation. He specifically stated that it was "not a result of works" (Ephesians 2:8-9). James clearly contradicts Paul in saying, people are "justified by works and not by faith alone" (James 2:24). As I understand it, this little contradiction was a major factor in what elicited Martin Luther's reformation. I am hardly qualified to toss this around with any meaningful result, but it does seem to be a rather important point of contention. I still cling to the idea that the Bible should be a very clear and concise guide to salvation and not a confusing mess of contradictions and questionable anecdotes that seem to make us notoriously fallible humans endlessly bump heads. That said, I feel obliged to recognize that it was also fallible humans who wrote scripture, compiled… by agenda… selected documents, and produced a Bible that doesn't seem to satisfy fellow believers of God and Jesus… as evidenced by myriad versions of it. What is a good agnostic supposed to do?

James also states that if a person submits to God, He will come nearer to that person… whatever that means. He warns about boasting, as well… though obviously not a sinful enough sin to be categorized as, perhaps, the eleventh commandment. He also encouraged patience, though he did not exactly say why. I can only guess that it was a vague reference to the second coming of Christ… but he did not say so. I'm not sure I am supposed to guess, though… that would be interpretation, and I think I have made it abundantly clear how I feel about that particular phenomenon.

November 6, 2013... Good For No Particular Reason

The Dalai Lama stated, in *The Art of Happiness*, that he believes people are born intrinsically good... the elusive definition of "good" notwithstanding. I happen to agree with this, but I really do not have anything concrete to base my stance on. I simply feel like I want to be moral and good and accepted and wanted and so on... and always have. Although I was certainly tutored from an early age to be good, and not bad, my tutors weren't exactly the best poster people for that particular cause. I have no doubts, though, that they wanted to be good, too... however successful they might have been in their efforts toward goodness. I have, in fact, never met a person who consciously declared a desire to be bad, though such a person might very well be out there somewhere. This general leaning toward goodness by virtually everyone... despite varying degrees of success, is compelling enough to me that I find myself fairly certain that what the Dalai Lama said is true.

So I want to be good... for my own satisfaction as well as the approval and acceptance of others. At least in my case, this declaration has nothing whatsoever to do with faith or God... or anything else. It is simply a feeling that I happen to harbor inside... and that I believe I was born with. My wife, and others, often say, "God is love." Without making a mess of that particular expression, I thought it might be interesting to think about how it might apply to my own "faith" that I am intrinsically good.

If I assume for a moment that God created me to be good, but with the capability to be bad, and with the unfortunate quirk that I can succumb to temptation (by Satan?), but with the ability to thwart him with no more than a conscious decision to do so (...and who wouldn't... considering the consequences?), then am I good? Can it be said that God created something (or someone) who is NOT good? ...or that MIGHT be good, pending good or bad works? Does good even matter at all? Paul said that it is only the acceptance of Christ as savior that would lead to salvation by God. James said to do good works, too.

What, exactly, is good anyway? I looked up good to see what the dictionary says. Definitions were more than a little vague. One even stated that good is a person who isn't bad... so now good is a person? I will attempt my own simple and clear definition of it: Good is having positive attributes or desirable qualities... good enough for me.

Now let's assume that God did not create me... good or otherwise... remembering that I feel like I was born basically good. How, then, did I acquire goodness? Earlier, when I talked about our intangible existences, I suggested that there is a possibility... however palatable it might seem to others, that our spirit could be a piece of some universally large gob of spirit in another dimension that we cannot readily detect with the senses we have... but that got captured by our brains (or assigned by...?) when we were born... or some time prior to that...that others can wrestle with. Or maybe our intangible consciousness was NOT a piece of a large gob, but instead, a separate and small intangible entity in another dimension that got too close when our brains happened to need an occupying life force. These ideas sound like whimsy... and maybe they are, but there is no harm in considering them. My point to all this is that wherever we happened to acquire our intangible existence from... from God or not from God, it appears to have positive attributes and desirable qualities (...although, admittedly, negative ones, too). So I am relegated to thinking of myself NOT as good or bad, but as more good than bad. Despite the urgings of others, I can't help but think that God, Himself, must also see us this way... since He made us both good and bad. It essentially HAS to be a matter of more good than bad, or more bad than good. Fortunately, for those of us who may have experienced, or caused, a streak of bad lately, we also have redemption as an ace up our sleeves. It appears to me that with an ounce of decision and a pound of sincerity... with a pinch of good works thrown in for flavor, we can attain our salvation in the Lord. That would be good.

There is one caveat, though. In what looks a bit like extortion to me, the Bible declares that judgment day is imminent... and anyone who hasn't taken the proverbial plunge into faith in Christ by that time limit... whenever it happens to be... will be too late and will forfeit salvation forever. In other words, we have been warned... do what is specified or suffer an eternal death in hell. In other words, do what is suggested or we will break your legs. So much for a "merciful" God.

November 11, 2013... Peter the Repeater

Peter's message, in 1 & 2 Peter, is an echo of the admonishments and exhortations of previous epistles. I can only suppose that the assemblers of the Bible saw that, by repetition, their Christian agenda would be seen as valid and convincing to readers of it... especially when considering the significant weight of a disciple's credential. I have to admit to a certain wonderment, myself... that an actual disciple of Jesus Christ left, not one, but two written letters describing his first-hand experience and knowledge of the Son of God... which has survived for two thousand years along with several other letters by the other disciples and apostles. These documents were assembled and published together to illustrate, no doubt, that the story and teachings of Christ were, indeed, believable and desirable to anyone wishing to find meaning for their lives. As stated earlier, though, it seems odd to me that so many contemporaries of Christ left concrete evidence of their lives and experiences and work, but there is nothing left from Christ Himself... other than His story as told by others. Although it is entirely possible for concrete evidence of a person's existence to be lost in time, there is, nevertheless, something a bit disturbing to me about the complete lack of any substantive, concrete evidence for the work of someone as important to humanity as Jesus Christ. How can it be that a Son of God, with the power over life and death, who was given to the world to communicate to us how salvation might be achieved... could do His lifetime's work, for the benefit of the entire human race (well, believers anyway), and leave no evidential trace whatsoever for future generations that might also feel a need for spiritual guidance. It seems entirely too convenient that these tales of wonder, meant to influence real human beings, are based on nothing more than faith... which has a substantial history of notoriously disastrous misdirection and genocidal consequences. God, Himself, was mightily disappointed with the performance of His own creation (us) more than once... according to the "inspired" words recorded in the Bible. How then, can He be satisfied with our acceptance of His Son... knowing as He must that we are still the same unreliable species He planted onto this earth. He obviously does NOT want all of us to be "saved"… or He would not have created a test to separate out the undesirables. He simply cannot convince me (in the very least) that He is concerned for the salvation of my soul when He has designed a system (in advance) that invariably will relegate many of us to Hell. Where, exactly, is the mercy in that.

Peter advises believers to submit to the authority and laws of the local governments. It seems to me that the Pharisees were admonished for that very thing. As with James, Peter seems to encourage believers to embrace suffering that is a result of good deeds… more so than for bad deeds (1 Peter 3:17). My feeling, though, is that suffering for doing good things is unjust… for any reason. If God sees the perseverance of suffering in His name as a good thing, then it looks to me that God has little power over bad things. As creator of the entire universe, should He not have the ability to simply snap His fingers and make both badness and suffering go away? If our spirits came from God, how can they be bad? How can they do bad things? Why didn't He just create us right? …and forego all this testing and unreliable faith-based salvation? If we humans had the ability to choose a spirit at birth that is good, why would anyone choose a bad or unreliable spirit knowing that God would send you to Hell for doing so? If we do not choose our spirits ourselves, then God must certainly have done it for us… so how can we be held responsible for our eventual failure in faith? If neither we, nor God, assigned us our spirits… and therefore our spiritual destinies, then it can be understood that God does NOT have jurisdiction over our spiritual choices. So what is going on here? None of the above scenarios appear to have any great validity to me. Are there more possibilities? Are we so unimaginative, as human beings that we cannot think up some sort of spiritual agenda that makes more sense? It looks to me that faith serves the faithful as ignorance is bliss.

November 12, 2013… A Break From Criticism

Lest I be seen as a hopeless atheist in my criticisms, I suppose I should reiterate what I pointed out some time ago. The familiar and time-worn phrases that I have encountered in the epistles, though disconcerting and hardly convincing in their dogma, are a comfort of sorts... in that, I have heard so very many of them through-out my life in church, songs, poems, and even, to be sure, everyday language. I am not naïve enough to be fooled by familiarity and repetition, however. Boiled down, the idea of faith is still troublesome to me in that the fate of my soul and the universe at large is supposedly at stake.

But there is something elusive and compelling in the New Testament that transcends my concerns, questions, and criticisms. I cannot say with any sort of conviction that I am being swayed by the famous writings, and I do not have much of a grasp on why it is somehow comforting to me, but I cannot deny that there is a draw... some kind of spiritual magnetism at work. I am probably much too prag-matic to succumb to it, but it is worth mentioning if I am to be completely honest in how the Work has affected me while I investigate its validity.

I should explain, though, that I am no C.S. Lewis. At this point in my quest for spiritual direction, I am still quite agnostic... unconvinced as ever. Lewis, to be fair, had powerful Christian adherents to contend with in his personal battle for spiritual fulfillment. His two best friends... one of which was my literary hero J. R. R. Tolkien, were devout and persistent influences on him. I have no such in-fluences hounding me... though in a way, I almost wish there were.

When my work is finished and all is considered, I still harbor hope that I will be spiritually able to rest at last... having had nothing these sixty-some years to afford intangible peace. My weariness from personal trials has taken its toll on me. It is not entirely out of the realm of possibility that I might wholehearted and gratefully accept the unsubstantiated salvation that a simple decision would offer me. Adversity might very well build character, but an unbearable and chronic long-term dose of it seems to make the content of my character of lesser importance than the much yearned for peace my soul is searching for. I am beginning to see how people can simply overlook the quirks of Christian teachings in order to enjoy the peace it promises... and which even the likes of me might find comforting, despite what I see as flaws.

November 13, 2013... A Word From the Anti-John

The three Books of John near the end of the New Testament are, again, letters written to encourage believers to be honest and committed in their belief. Although John echoes the preachings of his fellow Apostles, in many respects, he clearly exhorts the seriousness of real faith and the futility of apparent faith. There are also, as stated previously, familiar phrases that we modern Americans have all heard and come to know... and which, again, have a mysteriously comforting place in our spiritual space that I cannot put my finger on. He points out that Jesus was/is God's "only begotten Son" (1 John 4:9) and that "God is love" (1 John 4:8)... and he also describes the Holy Trinity as "Father, the Word, and the Holy Ghost: and these three are one."

Of all the familiar things I encountered in John's epistles, my only conspicuous point of contention concerns the idea of the Antichrist or Antichrists. This entity, or these entities, is mentioned nowhere else in the Bible. Certainly, there are references to Satan here and there... another entity I have issues with, but the Antichrist seems to be someone else... someone under the influence or jurisdiction of Satan, but who, according to John, is working in the world as a human deterrent to the works of Jesus. Although John is quite vague as to exactly who he is describing... he simply says that they are out there and doing their best to frustrate the works of Jesus. He is adamant, though, that we recognize them and avoid their influence... as true believers and "children of God" (1 John 3:10). Proponents of the Bible will likely explain that this reference to the Antichrist is, once again, an example of inspired scripture, but I find it more than a little disconcerting that John seems to have simply made up another contentious tale to further his agenda... good or bad though it may be. Something as important as an Antichrist, I should think, would have been at least mentioned elsewhere in the Bible. It was not. John is apparently the only inspired writer of scripture who was inspired enough to give mention about this particular little detail of faith and the possibility of eternal life. It seems fortunate... for us uninspired, but potentially Christian laymen, that it didn't go completely unmentioned. How many of us might have honestly and committedly followed one of these imposters to hell... though earnest in our belief? John said that that could not happen if we were earnest in our belief.

If we were "born of God", we would automatically be accepted into God's grace. This seems wonderful, but then who, exactly, was the Antichrist attempting to temp over to the dark side? He could not tempt the true children of God... they were true. He already had those who did not have an earnest belief commitment. Who is left? Agnostics? ...no such thing... one either wholeheartedly and earnestly believes, or one doesn't... according to John, himself, there is no middle ground. For what purpose, then, is there an Antichrist? ...and why has John simply over-looked people like me that are, indeed, undecided. ...and if I am undecided, am I automatically categorized as NOT "born of God"? Why then, are all those Christians out there trying to win me over when, according to John I am to be forsaken? Indeed, why were the Apostles, themselves, preaching to those not born of God unless, by their sincere acceptance of God, they might be saved? It looks to me like ordinary proponents of God, not to mention those of weaker convictions, have the power to completely deter Satan and the Antichrist... and with nothing more than a willing acceptance of Jesus. Rest assured, with an imminent sentence of eternal Hellfire awaiting me as an agnostic, I will quickly and seriously embrace Jesus Christ at some point... once I have strung Satan and His cohorts along for a time in a ruse of spiritual confusion.

November 14, 2013... Hey Jude

The epistle of Jude is very brief, and as such...nearly devoid of contestable issues. My only, admittedly weak, issue pertains to the previously discussed idea that in the New Testament Christian faith is supposedly based on the love of God... not the fear of God. Jude, however, reiterates the extortiony warning that judgment day is coming... and we better have our convictions in order...or else. He does, in all fairness, briefly mention that believers should look upon "doubters" as worthy of compassion... and therefore assistance toward faith in God. This statement alone allows me to view myself as a legitimate agnostic... despite how John ap-peared to view us, doubters. I am not sure, though, how one Apostle can say one thing and another something different... yet both are canonical and legitimate preachers of Jesus' doctrine. I, therefore, either will have a chance at salvation by way of Jude's epistle, or I won't because of John's insistence that one must whole-heartedly believe... or one simply doesn't... and is therefore either an Antichrist or one of his victims/lackeys.

In all honesty, I really cannot accept the Antichrist phenomenon at all... John or no John. There just doesn't seem to be any good reason for one to exist when Satan (whom I also have a problem with) seems to be perfectly capable of influencing anyone and everyone all at the same time and all by himself... sort of like God, Himself. Why would Satan feel the need to hire human lackeys to help him with the spoiling of mankind when God already established many times that humans are entirely unreliable and "stiff-necked". It seems that the wily Devil would like to tempt people into being even more unreliable than they already are... which, it seems to me, would make them poor choices for helpers. This reflects somewhat poorly on Satan's character, I should think.

November 22, 2013... Revelation Cogitation

After reading the Book of Revelation, my first inclination was to hark back to my earlier, regrettable, years as a practiced, hardcore, and ignorant fool in an effort to summarize my findings in a candid and entirely intentional derogatory way... probably with one word. I thought better of it though, and with measured effort, restrained myself out of respect for those who may have invested their time and money to share my thoughts. The least I should do, as a responsible journal writer, is provide some considered thoughts... if for no other reason than to illustrate that I do, indeed, occasionally have them.

I hardly know where to start. Anyone who may be following my progress through the Bible will certainly be aware of my tendency to be critical... to the best of my abilities as a Biblical layman, but Revelation is a book apart in my eyes. As much as the general intent of the book is meant to foretell prophecy, the wild and imaginative ludicrousness is almost beyond sensible comment. In the interest of respectful restraint, however, I will attempt a response that is perhaps more appropriate or palatable to readers who actually believe this...uh...stuff.

As I understand it, John, the protagonist in our story, is the disciple John... one of the Gospel authors. He has been selected by God to experience a vision of the future, incredible as it seems, and convey it to the churches... presumably as both a warning of doom and a promise of everlasting life. Then things get unquestionably weird. He sees the Son of Man with eyes like flames and who is holding seven stars that supposedly represent angels for the seven churches... which, themselves, are represented by seven candlesticks (naturally). The Son of Man regurgitates a two-edged sword. Then John is whisked off to the throne of God which is surrounded by twenty four "elders"... whatever they are supposed to be. Creatures with too many eyes and with faces like animals give glory to God. Then the lamb, being worthy, opens the seals on a scroll... whereupon multicolored horses ride forth with riders who are authorized to inflict various dooms upon the world. The sky disappears.

In chapter 7, four angels hold back the wind (even though there is no sky) and 144,000 servants of God are earmarked (forehead marked?) for a place in Heaven. These are broken up into groups of 12,000 from each of the twelve tribes of Israel (...no mention of all those gentiles who supposedly are also now eligible for salvation.) No mention of the tribe of Dan, either... one of the original twelve tribes. They seem to have gotten replaced by the house of Levi... who didn't count earlier.

Chapter 8 sees the seven angels blowing trumpets to loose their various dooms. One third of the land is scorched and one third of the sea turns red with blood (why only one third?). One third of the sun, moon, and stars go dark... even though the sky is already gone. Locusts are set upon the earth to torture everyone for five months... except the forehead-marked chosen ones. They look like horses with men's faces and with gold crowns on their heads. Four angels are released with their two hundred million cavalry troops to kill one third of all mankind. Another angel appears with a scroll that John is instructed to eat.

God then destroys the city (which one?) and one tenth of the people are killed... the rest repent... even though the time for repentance was supposedly over. In Chapter 12, a sign appears in the sky (that isn't there anymore) and a woman appears who gives birth to a son who a dragon with seven heads and ten horns wants to eat. War breaks out in Heaven. "A certain man" appears with the number 666 representing his name.

Angels pour out God's wrath from bowls onto the earth and Babylon is destroyed. The beast is thrown into the fiery pool. The dragon is chained and thrown into the abyss for a thousand years... but then he gets a pardon for a short time (?). After a thousand years, Satan is released (why?) then is thrown into a burning pool. All who were judged worthy are given a place in the new Heaven and Earth forever.

For most of my life, I had been fascinated by the idea of the apocalypse and Armageddon. Until these last few days, I had not read Revelation first hand and really had no good idea how the story went. Now I DO know how the story goes and I am, most definitely, not impressed. Even Peter Jackson couldn't make a credible movie of this book. It makes Stephen King books kid's stuff. It is totally preposterous in every way. There is nothing historical, believable, substantiatable, or earnestly and pragmatically meaningful here at all. If John had a dream, I would find it most difficult to accept that he could conjure up a ridiculous story like this. Two billion Christians or not, I'm not buying it. I have come to like the teachings of Christ. The Biblical morality, although quirky, is valid and appealing to me. Even the idea of a creator God is something I don't really have too much of a problem with... despite the lack of compelling proof or evidence. Revelation, though... in my lowly opinion, is decidedly not valid, not compelling, not historical, not believable, and not worth its questionable inclusion in the Great Book. It literally reads like the humorous imaginings of a four-year-old. Faith is one thing... difficult enough to master, but belief in the preposterous ridiculousness of Revelation is simply asking too much. I, therefore, refuse.

God supposedly created not only Heaven and Earth, but also Hell... for the eventual residence of His people, who He created, and who He made capable of failure, and for whom He made provisions for eternal damnation. Though I cannot proclaim that God does not exist (for I have no more proof of that than that He does), I can, with all due respect for the beliefs of others, wholeheartedly reject the Book of Revelation as the wildly, stupidly imaginative nonsense it appears to be. If I am wrong, I repent.

November 23, 2013... The Day After The End

I have now finished reading the Bible. I have commented honestly and openly about how the various parts of it affected me... and with the understanding that simply reading the Bible certainly does not make me an expert regarding it. I have very strong feelings about what I have encountered in the Book, and yet find my-self loathe to express them... out of a very real fear that I could easily lapse into disrespect... and be discredited, not for my debatable interpretations or misunderstood findings, but simply because I still harbor the tendency, after these sixty years, to characterize unpalatable things as…bull. I do not, however, wish to do that. One of the reasons I have taken on the daunting challenge of a personal Biblical investigation is that I no longer want to be who I used to be. I don't want to be as ignorant as I was. I don't want to live the remainder of my life ignoring the very real intangible existence that I... and all of us... have. I don't want to be crude or mean or disrespectful or condescending anymore.

I had hoped that upon finishing the New Testament, I would have some sort of enhanced understanding of spirituality... some kind of direction to go, spiritually... that might eventually lead me to (excuse the overused phrase) inner peace. I actually thought, somewhere back in some little-used storage closet, that what happened to C.S. Lewis…might happen to me. As I mentioned earlier, I really am quite emotionally and spiritually weary. Although sixty one years old, I feel like a two-year-old spiritually; "I want. I want. I want."

Honestly, I knew going into this project, that I would likely find few, if any, answers. I fully understand that faith is not based on proofs or evidence... or even validity…really. And I know full well that faith is something that I can wield as much as anyone, but I am resolute in my desire to avoid ignorance as best I can... and assemble some variation of faith that is sensible from my point of view, helpful... in at least a limited way... with my emotional weariness and valid enough to be worth pursuing…and gratefully acceptable.

What I have found, instead, is never-ending bias, an almost unbelievable willingness, by nearly everyone, to ignore the idiosyncrasies, contradictions, and just plain silliness that riddles the Bible. Unsubstantiated justifications are seen as proofs. Opinions are taken as truths. The writings of man are accepted as the words of God, when other writings of man are not... and with nothing more to go on than what is written.

I do not mean to say that the Bible is ALL questionable. To be sure, there is certainly as many, or more, good things to say...as bad. The historicity is obvious and compelling... quirky as it is. The morality is unquestionably tantamount and simply cannot be underappreciated by a reasonable person. Even the Book, itself, has to be considered a masterpiece of literature... having had the impact it has on the entire world for hundreds of years... despite my many, perhaps esoteric, misgivings.

So now what? Although I expected my quest for spiritual validity to be near an end, I now find that I must continue searching. There are, and have been, simply far too many people who have accepted the Christian dogma for me to discount the validity of it on my findings alone. I believe it is time to introduce, and investigate, the opinions of others into my spiritual soup. With luck, a small tidbit of something-or-other will inexplicably resonate within me. ...something I missed, or something I misunderstood. Perhaps there really are seven-headed creatures with ten horns and man-faces and bowls of doom out there...and I just missed it somehow. I am willing to admit that I am wrong. I am more than willing to repent all of my sins... already have. I am willing to learn a better way if one can be found. I am happy to share my thoughts with anyone open-minded enough to realize that my thoughts are mine... not meant to influence anyone else... and not a basis for judgments about others. If God is out there... and He very well may be, then He surely must know my mind (if I remember my Bible)... and therefore understand my good intentions and inadvertent failings...since He supposedly made them for me... and me for them.

November 25, 2013... Beetlejuice, Beetlejuice, Beetlejuice

I was thinking today about how, exactly, I might expand my search for a spiritual path for my intangible existence. I had hardly thought the thought when I recalled

the wonderful movie Beetlejuice... and the similar predicament that our protagonists experienced with the perplexing realization that they had died. They did not
know what they should do next... a feeling I can identify with. Whereas they were
able to call upon the services of the self-proclaimed spiritual guide for help... however mistakenly, I do not have that luxury. And since, as I stated previously, I tend
to think better when I write, I am anxiously awaiting whatever inspiring thoughts
I will think...to manifest themselves. I'm ready.

One of my overriding concerns is a desire to find unbiased sources of information that I can digest on my own terms... that is, without the invariable pressure
of others pushing their own agendas or beliefs my way. This alone will be a considerable challenge since I know of no one who is unbiased. I know of no information sources that are unbiased...and who is qualified to judge bias, anyway? I
suppose the best I can hope for is to investigate myriad sources of information,
bias and all, and then find some average, or middle ground, that works for me.

One thought I toyed with a few months ago, was to assemble a group of friends
and acquaintances... who are intelligent enough to respect my reasons for gathering
them together... and with differing views on spirituality or Christianity...and have
a discussion. This is not something I would do lightly since few of my friends know
that I ponder these lofty ideas at all. If they truly are friends, though, I should
think a brief explanation would put them more at ease. The idea would be to host
a group of (hopefully) free and critical thinkers who would provide various views
on whatever spiritually-related topics might be expressed... with an emphatic insistence on a peaceful and respectful discussion. Although I, personally, feel this
would be an interesting and possibly enlightening private event, even a group of
my carefully chosen, and highly respected, friends will likely get no further toward
definitive answers than I was able to get on my own. A valid direction for my
intangible existence is my goal... not necessarily specific, though esoteric, answers
to life's nagging questions. There is likely nothing to be gained by such a discussion. If I was bolder, and perhaps more learned regarding these spiritual ideas, I
might solicit a more qualified and credentialed group in hopes of actually getting
somewhere with the effort. Two thousand years of study, debate, argument, and
war, however, indicates otherwise.

December 7, 2013... Pursuing Positivity

My pretty wife, who also happens to be no fool, noticed early on that I was an unfortunate example of human failings. Fortunately, for me though, her love and empathy allowed her to see inside of me to some extent... where the buried little boy resided... the one with the real feelings. She simply knew that there was some value in me... despite my sometimes questionable behaviors and lack of real outward respect. It is largely for her that I repent my sins and failings... primarily because she was the unfortunate primary recipient of them. To be sure, I suffered, as well... not only for experiencing the consequences of my quirky actions, but because somewhere, deep inside, I was starting to realize that my soul was broken... perhaps beyond repair. Whereas I had been able, in my younger years, to allow humor, escapism, and fun to hide my inner turmoil, as I aged, I became more sour, dour, and negative in my demeanor. This is not to say that I wasn't able to cover it all up for others. I did. But when things quieted down at home and I felt I could be "real"... the real me emerged; depressed, angry, mixed up, and inaccessible. What is worse, as I said earlier, this was all quite normal and beyond any reasons for action on my part. I simply did not understand how existing the way I did could be wrong... much less hurtful to others. Surely others would realize that we are all a result of our inescapable fates. My inner angst was of no more concern (to me) than anyone else's. I, therefore, did nothing about myself for most of my life.

I am embarrassed to confess on these pages that I have not rectified my negativity problem to this day. To be sure, I am certainly working on it... diligently journaling and mulling possibilities and practicing self-awareness, but I have not succeeded to an acceptable degree. Neither me, nor my wife, can rest easy with the confidence that I will not fold into myself at any time. Of all of the intangible obstacles I have wrestled with during the past ten years, this nagging negative side of me has been the most frustrating to deal with. ...and that is only from my perspective... others, my wife, in particular, have also suffered because of me.

I have been told that one method that can be used to counter the dread of negativity is the fake it until you make it method. I honestly don't know if that actually works, but there doesn't seem to be any downside to making the attempt.

I am constantly reminded that my negativity probably affects me more than anyone else... so why do I allow myself to manifest it? This is a sixty-year-old habit that was pressure-drilled into me from an early age. Its mitigation is most certainly easier said than done.

I asked myself, "What, exactly, is my negativity about?" Obviously, it isn't an easy nut to crack, but then not cracking that nut means not fixing my problem. It occurs to me that I need something. It would be simple to name the obvious things: love, touch, happiness, peace, popcorn... But why would I allow myself to be victimized by myself in my manifestation of need? I don't have answers, but I can only surmise that I revert back to some sort of infant response when the need becomes more than I can understand and cope with. With this in mind, I have begun to use self-awareness to catch my negative side from getting a foothold on my day. It doesn't always work, but it is better than suffering the sixty-year curse for another sixty years.

For several years, I accepted escapism as a valid deterrent... and I still think it can help. Many times I have lost myself in a television movie and found myself feeling better for a while. Reading is also quite helpful at bedtime when the lights go down and the nagging, pinching night crawls into bed with me. Sleep usually comes in snippets and the morning lays heavy on me most of the time. At some point, morning, midday, or evening, I am forced to come to terms with myself... and simply decide to feel better. It doesn't always work, but sometimes it does.

My wife, meanwhile, has become deserving of extra credit.

December 19, 2013... Hoping, Coping, and Moping

Sometimes my own problems and concerns... esoteric and slippery as they are... seem overwhelming to me, and as such are frustratingly, and chronically, burdensome. But there are more than a few instances of adversity lately that are causing financial hardships, emotional stresses and psychological exhaustion for some of my acquaintances. These things weigh heavy on me these days as, in recent years, I am more able to feel adversity more than ever before... and empathize with those afflicted with it. I seldom know, or even consider, what to do about these people...

not surprising since I, likewise, don't know what to do about myself, but I feel for them nonetheless.

My wife points out that the severity of other people's problems can be used to minimize the apparent severity of my own. Although I understand this reasoning, it actually does nothing to make me feel better... despite how earnestly she believes this will work. In actuality, it only serves to add to my feeling that adversity is ubiquitous, chronic, and often beyond mitigation. ...and this kind of thinking probably feeds the all-too-common depression in people.

There are times when I will simply become fed up with it all and declare, inwardly, that I am not going to let myself be victimized by my own negativity anymore. I can feel a little strength in that kind of thinking, but it doesn't last. My newly learned self-awareness tells me that I have apparently built myself a nice little baseline box to live in that fits rather well, but which prevents me from leaving my comfort zone and actually fixing something. The walls I built around myself not only keep more troubles out, but also the fixes for them. They not only keep my sanity safely within their confines, but also my suppressed ability to flex my psychological muscles toward personal improvements. I suppose we all do that to some extent... right or wrong, but making excuses for it doesn't help things.

So how, exactly, does one constructively deal with this never-ending onslaught of adversity? What can someone like me actually do about it? I have encountered one possibility that sort of fits with the idea behind this book. People have said, "Why don't you try prayer?" ...or, "I'll pray for you." ...or, "God has a plan for you... even if you don't understand what it is." But there is also this: "God helps those who help themselves." ...and, "...suffering produces perseverance; perseverance, character; and character, hope." (Romans 5:3-5) Do I embrace my personal adversity in the interest of making points with God? ...or do I avoid it like the plague, tune in to The Lord of the Rings trilogy, make some popcorn, and sort of sail away for a while? Personally, I prefer the latter.

I would probably do myself an injustice if I was to limit my options to the ones above. Surely there are other ways to deal with the sometimes debilitating effects of adversity. As I think I mentioned earlier in this work, the Dalai Lama suggested the use of adversity as a catalyst to make something better. With practice, we apparently can begin to see adversity as a borderline desirable... the first step in a process that ends with the successful improvement of something in our lives... and although this sounds like a good thing, I personally cannot help but see the trouble as the trouble it is... despite the benefits it can inspire. Right or wrong, I still see the intentional avoidance of adversity as a viable and probably sensible course of action... or inaction. If a bully, in his characteristic best form, fires a hard and accurate snowball at my face, I WILL duck... and no psychological or spiritual reason for NOT ducking will make me consider other possibilities.

The Dalai Lama also suggested, in the Art of Happiness, that we can learn to simply repel adversity "like water runs off a duck's back." In essence, the idea is that we can convince ourselves that adversity has very little power over us... and simply ignore it, or minimize it to some minor significance. This, I will admit, intrigues me. Anyone who has been around me for the last ten years or so will likely recognize my well-practiced and often used response to many of the negatives that have challenged me: "Oh well." This, though, is more of a response to adversity than a way of dealing with it... although it is still effective and useful.

I have also found over the years that, in my own case, simply letting go of life's little negative surprises works... at least to some degree... as well as anything. There have been times when my wife and I experienced unpleasantness, usually blew it out of proportion, and then, after a time, essentially agreed to let it go in the interest of getting along. Nothing was fixed, but the effect of the adversity was minimized... and the head butting ceased. Although probably not the best course of action when real problem solving might have been called for, avoidance proved at least partially beneficial once again. The Dalai Lama's suggestion of ignoring the negativity to minimize its effects seems valid... at least sometimes.

The idea that one might pray for deliverance from troubles, in my eyes, seems to be a variation of avoidance therapy (as I call it). God will intervene or help us through somehow... supposedly... thereby taking the pressure off of us. God, however, created this mess though... if I'm not mistaken. ...or maybe it was Satan. Either way, we were apparently meant to experience adversity in our lives. So praying to God for mitigation... or Satan, for that matter, seems fruitless to me. If we were not meant to experience troubles, troubles would not have been created for us by our creator... and if God did not create our troubles, then apparently we have more than one creator to deal with... like I said, it's a mess.

One of my most excruciating and perplexing banes in life has to do with how I, personally, react to adversity. I simply do not do it very well... and it appears to me that others are, likewise, underqualified to deal with it, as well. I mope...and hold on to psychological duress for far too long. It is not a matter of simply being moody, or even mildly depressed, it is a well-practiced and often used manifestation of self-abuse. I know I do it. I know I should stop doing it, but as I said...it is a well-established, deep-seated habit that affects others as well as me. Coping with it is not enough. Avoiding it is not consistently possible or effective. I find it difficult to ask a creator for help when He "created the heaven and the earth." (Genesis 1:1) Somehow, I feel that I must learn how to both minimize and tolerate the inescapable and never-ending string of troubles that come my way...on my own. No one else seems any more capable, willing, or qualified to offer valid help than I am... but maybe I am a bit arrogant in that claim. So far, so bad.

January 23, 2014... A Fork In The Road

Cunning and observant readers of this manuscript will have noticed the month that has passed since my last effort at constructive and meaningful self-discourse. There is a reason for it...besides what is known here in the Midwest as "the Holidays". In truth, I am at an impasse. I am most disappointed that my critical reading of the Bible, as a curious, serious, and hopeful layman, produced no discernible change in my self-described status as agnostic. I still consider the existence of God as...as much a possibility as any other idea we humans might come up with rightfully or wrongly. The Bible did not convince me in the least that its message is...well...the gospel... compelling though it is. I acknowledge passion, history, eloquent prose, and imaginative, perhaps, wishful thinking, but I encountered no proofs, no conspicuous truths, no evidence-based direction for me to follow... spiritual or otherwise. However wrongly I may be taken, I saw hearsay. I do not accept that, by virtue of the written word, proof is established. It is likely that I might be denigrated for this thinking, but whether misguided or not, it is honest.

So now I have traveled a long and winding literary road only to come upon a fork... the one everyone comes to sooner or later, and with no signs to point which way I should go from here. If I go one way, I will trend towards atheism... with no more established and proven reason to go that way than any other. If I go the other way, I will embrace theism... again, with no verifiable and undeniable evidence to support that decision. If I go back, I will simply wallow in a vast pond of uncertainty that I have already waded across.

I have been accused at times of being imaginative, creative, and resourceful. Questionable as it might be, it occurs to me that, as is typically the case, there may be other possibilities... regarding faith, that I simply have not encountered yet. The spiritual realm appears to be a universe that may be as vast as the physical one we are beginning to find ourselves in. The physics of that intangible universe seems to largely elude us, despite our insistence that we understand what we can't see... and believe in what we can't know. I could simply choose a belief... accept what others are adamant about, and live accordingly, but I am weary of ignorance and more than willing to define or acknowledge it... in an effort to avoid or mitigate it. I don't mind being ignorant if ignorance is the refusal to give in to popular or widespread ideas based solely on unverifiable faith. I cannot see magnetism, yet I know it is there. It can be substantiated by its effect on other objects... and it can be harnessed as a power source. I cannot see most of the electromagnetic radiation spectrum, yet I know it is there. The infrared cooks my toast. The X-rays leave a picture of my bones on a sheet of vellum. The unseen can be substantiated given enough time to discover or invent detectors. I have to think that the spiritual side of our existence is just such a thing... wanting of a detector that hasn't been dreamed of yet ...a challenging and eminently interesting frontier that has not been breached... yet. I see no reason to justify our ignorance by embracing ideas that are based on nothing more than our historically skewed and quirky view of things we know little or nothing about.

I am not giving up. Fully fifty percent of my existence is a total mystery to me... and I don't like it. But I also don't like the baseless acceptance of passionate wishful thinking... however universal the thinking might seem. Faith might be considered a worthwhile and desirable pastime, and there are obviously some benefits to it, but until someone presents me with a more valid reason to practice it than its time-tested acceptance and the Bible's status as a self-legitimized resource, I need more. My search will go on. I will find a direction for a continued search... if not my spiritual leanings. Agnosticism, however well-meant, is (in my opinion) for quitters who aren't willing to pursue what they don't understand. They declare an Agnostic impasse... and leave it at that. I cannot accept that way of thinking. I cannot leave fully fifty percent of my existence in a state of defeated ignorance. We who profess to be agnostics should be the spearheads of earnest attempts to find meaning where there doesn't appear to be any. We should find a way to use our skepticism and inquisitive natures as a catalyst to discover a detector that will substantiate SOMETHING on the intangible side of things. Not knowing is, if you will pardon the expression, Hell. ...and I don't like it.

I believe I stated around the beginning of this investigation that I had hopes for finding valid reasons for a sincere and permanent conversion to, or acceptance of, the Christian faith... as C.S. Lewis famously (and reluctantly) did in his Surprised By Joy. Again, I am no C.S. Lewis, whether in literary merit or dogmatic study, but I will graciously admit to reluctance in my continued status as Agnostic... as established by this fifteen-month layman's reading of the Holy Bible. I will herewith declare a continued willingness to consider Christian thinking, but I will also move on. Possibilities, by their very nature, are everywhere and probably never-ending. How can a sincere and open-minded person of spiritual curiosity and need be content with the study of only one possibility?

I fear the likelihood of never-ending searches for the meaning of intangible existence. I find it excruciatingly frustrating that the overused, but under-explained, "inner peace" is so elusive. As I look earnestly and honestly for clues to the meaning of life, I also inadvertently find ubiquitous and exasperating ignorance and intolerance. This sort of search for validity in faith necessarily requires a certain respect for the beliefs of others... a challenge in itself, but the requirement is noted and the effort will continue to be made with a willing consideration for what I see as the mostly inherent good of the human race... and if I die before I wake, I pray the Lord my soul to take.

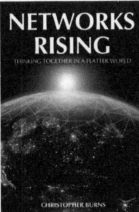